"If you lead at any level in today's disrupted and crazy world, read these books on modern management. As with all Johanna's books, they are full of insightful stories, real world examples and concrete actionable advice. Use these books to guide your own development, support and lead others, and guide your organisation to greater success."

—SHANE HASTIE, DIRECTOR OF COMMUNITY DEVELOPMENT ICAGILE

"Each product team has its own culture. It is important for leaders to understand where culture comes from and how they can influence it so that their teams can build better products. In the *Modern Management Made Easy* books, Johanna Rothman has some valuable advice to help you be more purposefully create a culture that will support the team while driving powerful innovations. Her style of writing includes questioning and addressing industry myths that draw from decades of real world experience. Her work will change the way you lead product."

—SEAN FLAHERTY, EVP OF INNOVATION AND COHOST OF
THE PRODUCT MOMENTUM PODCAST.

"With her characteristic blend of pragmatism, insight, and wit, Johanna Rothman takes on the role of modern management's mirror, mythbuster, and mentor. The first in her *Modern Management Made Easy* trilogy, *Practical Ways to Manage Yourself* demystifies the illusions we knowledge workers spin. Offering thought-provoking observations from her own career, along with steps to help identify and replace outmoded thinking and habits while gently urging guiding the reader towards a more thoughtful management practice, this latest volume reinforces why Johanna remains among modern management's most readable, relevant, and respected thinkers."

—TONIANNE DeMARIA, COAUTHOR OF SHINGO-AWARD WINNING
Personal Kanban

Practical Ways to
Lead an Innovative Organization

Modern Management Made Easy: Book 3

Johanna Rothman

Practical Ink

Arlington, Massachusetts

Practical Ways to Lead an Innovative Organization
Modern Management Made Easy: Book 3

Johanna Rothman

Published by Practical Ink
www.jrothman.com

Practical **ink**

Cover design: Brandon Swann, swanndesignstudio.com
Cover art: Company Value Icons by Angela Cini, on depositphotos.com

Ebook: 978-1-943487-18-9
Print: 978-1-943487-19-6
Hardcover: 978-1-943487-20-2

In memory and honor of Jerry Weinberg who told me I should write a book about rewiring management logic.

For Edward Rothman, my first management mentor.

And, for Mark, Shaina and Adam, and Naomi and Matt, as always. Thank you for managing me.

Contents

CHAPTER 11

Don't People Already Know How to Do Their Jobs? . . . 119

CHAPTER 12

Doesn't Lower Salaries Mean Lower Project Cost? 127

CHAPTER 13

Who Has the Power to Decide?. 137

CHAPTER 14

Isn't the Organization a Well-Oiled Machine? 153

CHAPTER 15

Where's the Quick Fix or Silver Bullet? 167

List of Figures

Acknowledgments

I thank all the people who read and commented on the management myths columns as I wrote them. I also thank Software Quality Engineering, now known as Techwell, who first published these columns.

I thank my coaching and consulting clients. You have taught me more than you know.

I thank my technical reviewers: Matt Barcomb, Pawel Brodzinski, Andrea Goulet, Mark Kilby, Leland Newsom.

I thank Rebecca Airmet for her editing. I thank Brandon Swann for his cover design. I thank Karen Billipp for her layout and Jean Jesensky for her indexing.

Any mistakes are mine.

Introduction

Several years ago, I wrote a series of articles I called "management myths." They each described how I'd seen managers act so that the manager created the opposite result from the one they wanted. Yes, the manager's actions created precisely the opposite effect.

I wrote a myth a month for 36 months.

I assumed as the world transitioned to agile approaches or approaches where teams, managers, and organizations needed more resilience, that managers would change. I thought no one needed to read about the myths in a world where we want collaborative, cross-functional, self-managing teams.

I was wrong.

As I worked with more managers who wanted to use agile approaches, I realized these problems:

- Existing management practices didn't work at all for agile teams or teams that need to exhibit adaptability and resilience.
- Those practices didn't work for managers who wanted to lead and serve others.
- These practices actively prevented innovation.

Leaders, teams, and innovators succeeded despite their management.

And, in an organization attempting to transform to an agile culture? The more the managers tried to make old patterns work, the less agility anyone exhibited.

Why did these smart people behave in ways that didn't make sense?

They didn't know they had options.

These managers had never witnessed useful management, never mind excellent management. They tried to do the best job they could. And, they perpetuated what they'd experienced, or possibly even learned in school. They practiced what they'd seen—the old ways of management.

It's time for real modern management.

Modern managers have enormous challenges. They feel as if they are between the proverbial rock and a hard place.

How can you become a modern manager when the system, the culture, is based on old thinking and old practices?

Carefully.

I've divided the original essays into three books. Book 1, *Practical Ways to Manage Yourself*, asks you to consider how you can manage and respect yourself to build congruence and integrity in your actions.

Book 2, *Practical Ways to Lead and Serve (Manage) Others*, explains how you can serve a harmonic whole. The entire team or group can then work together in a culture of transparency and trust.

This third book explores ways to create a human and innovative culture in your organization, so you can use the ideas of trust and integrity to create a place where people want to work.

You might feel many constraints in your situation. As you read these books, you might nod and say, "Yes, I can do that." And, you might shake your head at some ideas and say, "Not going to touch that here. Nope, not at all."

I do hope you consider each essay as a possible experiment for your management practice. You have options.

Who Are the People in These Essays?

You might wonder about my use of names and gender in these books. For example, you might never have seen women as senior managers. I have seen men and women as senior managers. I've been a senior manager.

My experience tells me that a given gender does not equate to great or unfortunate management skills. Neither does a person's country of origin or any other kind of individual demographic.

To help you see what the management world could be, I've created parity across genders. I've used names of people I've worked with or admired. Even with that, I've changed all the names to protect the innocent and the guilty.

I've had the good fortune to meet and work with male and female managers worldwide. In almost every circumstance, the managers have done the best they could, given their company's environment and culture. The manager's gender didn't matter.

The company's environment mattered more than anything. You might—or might not—see the variety of people in roles that I write about here.

Through my work, I've recognized several principles that create great management and build healthy organizational cultures.

1. Clarify purpose—for you, the team, and the organization.
2. Build empathy with the people who do the work.
3. Build a safe environment. People work better when they can trust you, their colleagues, and the organization as a whole.
4. Seek outcomes by optimizing for an overarching goal.
5. Encourage experiments and learning.

6. Catch people succeeding.
7. Exercise value-based integrity as a model for the people you lead and serve.

All three books build on these principles:

- Respect—for yourself, for the team, and for the purpose of the organization.
- Trust—possibly with boundaries—to encourage the behaviors and outcomes you want.
- Team-based approaches to working at all levels of the organization.

All three books explain some of the trickier parts of management. You'll get the most value if you read all three books.

As you read the dialogue in the essays, remember that I said most of these things to my managers. You might see these conversations as insubordination.

I didn't feel as if I was insubordinate. I used the principle of congruence to have conversations where my manager and I cared about the outcome, each other, and discovered our best possible outcome for the situation.

You and I are different people. How I frame conversations might not work for you. You will find *your* best ways to describe the situation and influence your manager.

You can practice human and humane management that produces superior results for your organization. You can respect yourself, the people you serve, and the entire organization as well as customers. You can act with integrity. And, you can have empathy without being a pushover.

You might worry—will you still be able to obtain the necessary financial results you want? Yes, innovative leaders create an environment that balances short-term needs—including financial—with a culture of innovation and change.

Management is an honorable profession. We need managers—

great, congruent managers who can use their interpersonal skills to get the best out of themselves first. Then, they can extend those skills to the people they serve and across the organization.

This book is about how you might create an environment that promotes innovation. I'll suggest many options you can consider to ease your management and encourage innovation.

Let's start.

CHAPTER 1

Encourage Management Innovation

Have you ever seen innovation in a management team?

Think back to your participation in innovative teams, groups, or organizations. Aside from the fun and challenge, you had a specific common goal. You and your team focused on that single goal. Everyone contributed as they could to the goal—and people learned from each other. All the participants understood the state of the work. And you were able to show other people your work.

The team had sufficient autonomy to work in ways that suited them—for their internal process and inside the organization. And, the team produced. They were able to show interim progress internally. Depending on the product or service, they integrated feedback loops from other people across the organization and customers.

Each innovative team or group I've worked with has had a different feel. Some of them socialized at work. Some didn't. Some encouraged loud disagreements. Others had a culture of only library-loud voices.

The teams managed their working agreements for their behaviors and actions. And, I've seen each innovative team—including innovative management teams—exhibit these innovation principles.

1.1 Consider These Innovation Leadership Principles

If you want to lead an innovative organization, consider these principles:

1. Clarify purpose. Why does your organization exist? What customers does it serve? What problems does it solve?
2. Build empathy with the people who do the work. Examine your policies and procedures—do they help people do the work or hinder the people?
3. Build a safe environment. How safe are you to exercise your integrity, disagree with others, prioritize the work, and more? Do you clarify why and when you make decisions and what to do when people disagree?
4. Seek outcomes by optimizing for an overarching goal. When managers work in flow efficiency, they optimize for the organization, not their department or themselves.
5. Encourage experiments and learning. The more innovation you want, the more everyone will need to experiment and learn.
6. Catch people succeeding. Create small-world networks where people can offer each other reinforcing feedback and learn together.
7. Exercise your value-based integrity. When the managers and the organization's policies work with integrity, people notice. They will make more decisions that you want and fewer decisions you don't want.

You'll notice I didn't include transparency or communication in these principles. That's because if you use all these principles, you will communicate more effectively. You will be as transparent as you can be with the people you serve.

When I've been a part of innovative teams and organizations, they used these principles. They experimented, learning as they proceeded. They were able to learn and extend the organization's products, services, and knowledge.

Notice that all these principles rely on human relationships. That's why the ideas in Books 1 and 2 are so critical to effective management and leading an innovative organization. When managers create the environment for human relationships to thrive, the organization can innovate.

And, because relationships are the heart of innovation, these innovative teams are—surprisingly—fragile. If someone from outside the team or group meddles in the team—changes any of these characteristics—the relationships falter and eventually die. (That someone might be you, your peer manager, or other managers in the hierarchy.) The innovative team cannot sustain its innovation.

External meddling breaks the necessary relationships between the team members and their contacts outside the specific team.

I've seen well-meaning managers challenge every single innovation principle. The managers don't define an overarching purpose, so people don't see the meaning in what they do. The managers ask the members to multitask or the manager looks for milestones, not outcomes you can see. Or, the manager asks people to work alone, isolated in their silo or cubicle.

Worse, I've seen too many organizations say that people are their greatest asset. Then, these same managers don't act to optimize the environment for the people. The managers actively discourage experimentation with policies, procedures, and mandates. And, the managers make decisions—and no one understands why.

Why do managers act this way? Often, because they fear risks or potential problems—or the manager does not feel safe. Instead of clarifying and explaining their fears, the managers became conservators of the status quo. They don't encourage change and experimentation to discover a new status quo.

Here's a quick test to see if your organization rewards conservator, status quo thinking: Does the organization reward success as measured by following plans, not learning from experiments? If so, you work in a more conservator-oriented organization.

When we work in conservator mode, we protect the institution from immediate failure. We ingrain current modes of working that don't allow for and encourage change. We stagnate.

When we work in experiment mode, we learn and extend what the institution can do.

Managers and leaders struggle to find the "right" balance between protection and experimentation. That balance changes with the market context and with the people in the organization.

In my experience, both conservators and experimenters have the best interests of the organization at heart. (Yes, there is a small set of cynics in many organizations who only want to satisfy their self-interest. However, most people I meet want their organizations to succeed.)

Our organizations need innovation now more than ever. Peter Drucker said this in *The Essential Drucker* [DRU01]:

> ". . . every organization—not just businesses—needs one core competence: *innovation*."

And, Gary Hamel said "Management innovation . . . yields a competitive advantage" [HAM07].

If you manage for innovation, you manage *for* change. To encourage change, you need to know your organization's purpose— why your organization exists.

1.2 **Start With Why**

Why is your organization in business? I'm not talking about the "excellence" or "delivery" or any of that buzzword bingo nonsense. Do you know which customers you serve and why? How about your employees? Why does your organization exist?

Too often, I see the organization's leaders say they deliver value to the shareholders. Or that they focus on the short-term and making money.

Every company needs money to fund its work.

However, making money is not a mission. Neither is creating value for the shareholders. Companies make money and create value for the shareholders as an outcome of creating products and services customers love.

Companies use their purpose to decide which products and services to offer. That purpose, through the products and services, attracts employees and customers. The purpose helps create the environment.

When I work with managers about their why, I ask questions such as these:

- What is your purpose, the difference you will make in the world?
- Why do people care about that difference?

As Simon Sinek says in *Start with Why* [SIN09], "People don't buy WHAT you do, they buy WHY you do it." When you start to explore your why, you can see how you can attract employees and customers.

When you know your why, everyone pulls together—because they all believe in the same purpose.

The purpose helps the organization frame possible innovations as experiments. (Any given experiment might fail—the success occurs when people learn from their work.) Not trivial experiments that allow us to relearn gravity, but experiments with management, with products, and with the processes we use. Great experiments help us learn a lot in a short period of time.

When managers spend time defining why *their* organization is different, they can attract their ideal customers—and ideal employees. Those ideal customers start and continue to buy, funding the organization. And, those customers tell their friends and colleagues. The employees help the organization recruit other great employees.

The organization makes money as an *outcome* of finding and exploiting your difference as an organization—your organization's "why." And, why defines the meaning people want for their jobs.

People Want Work to Matter

A senior manager, Jim, told me, "None of the people here care about meaning in their work. We're all in it for the big bucks."

I asked what he rewarded. Did he reward meaning, or did he reward delivering the same kind of products again and again?

"The products," he said.

I asked, "How many of your best people went to your competitors or other organizations where they can learn and grow?" I knew they had about 25% turnover the previous year.

He growled and walked away.

He worked for the money. He didn't care about the customers, the products, or the employees.

You might think only a particular generation works for meaning. Not true. While I've met cynical people like Jim, I've met many more people who work *for* meaning.

Jim had only worked for managers who trained everyone to work for money and self-interest, not for meaning.

When people work for self-interest, they use their employment to make life as comfortable as possible for themselves, before and after retirement. People who work in their self-interest are incongruent with others and the organization.

You may know or work with people who don't care about meaning in their work. I bet it's because they don't feel safe to explore what the meaning might be. Or, they tried—for years—to find meaning, and now they're working for a paycheck.

It's not worth their trouble and time to find meaning at work. These people find meaning elsewhere—in their community, in a sport, in their family.

If you pay those people enough, they'll stay with your organization for long enough, maybe even many years. They'll do what you ask. That's a transactional relationship to the work.

If you've seen this transactional relationship before, you might think these people need motivation. (No one lacks motivation. All motivation is internal.) Instead, consider how you can act to stop *demotivating* the cynics and transactional workers.

People need you to trust them to do work within reasonable boundaries. They will, if you also offer meaning in the work.

If you don't know your "why"—why the organization exists—you can't offer meaningful work. And, if you can't align the people to work on an overarching goal, you still can't offer meaningful work.

Most people have a why for their careers which helps them choose one job over another. And, that why doesn't have to be the same as the organization's why. However, the two whys do need to intersect enough so the organization's why invites the person to do their best job.

Everyone's motivation eventually withers without meaning. When people don't see meaning, they do what the manager tells them to do. These people stop thinking. They don't consider any kind of change.

Your organization's "why" frames its common goals and shared values—the meaning people find at work. That meaning allows everyone to be effective.

1.3 Manage for Effectiveness

Many organizations prize efficiency. Efficiency is different from effectiveness.

- When we are efficient, we take the extra steps and waste out of the work.
- When we manage for effectiveness, we first decide which work to do and not do.

When we start with efficiency, we might do the wrong work quite well. That doesn't help fulfill our "why." In a real sense, we waste time on the wrong work.

Instead, when we start with effectiveness, we make the difficult decisions about what to do and when to do it. Those decisions help us continue to refine what makes us effective for our customers and employees—what fulfills our "why."

I've met too many managers who think they need to manage for efficiency. The managers want to standardize the process, measures, and tools. They want to measure and reward individual work. The managers believe they are efficient.

To be fair, many business schools still teach this approach to management. If you were taught this and believe it, you are in good company.

However, managing knowledge work for efficiency ignores the fact that effective knowledge work requires people to learn together. Learning together is rarely efficient.

I have to admit. I love my *personal* efficiencies. I organize my work and my personal life, to waste few movements. My system works for *me*. My efficiencies don't "scale" even to my family.

It's the same for the people you lead and serve.

When we first look for efficiency, we treat people as if they are cogs in a machine. We use a mechanistic approach to management— we ignore our human relationships at work.

When we don't acknowledge the humanity of the workplace, we create a system that produces a race to the bottom. The system starts a downward spiral of losing the best employees and then, the best customers. At some point, you don't have a growing, innovative organization.

If we want innovative organizations, we first need to decide why we're in business. Then, we decide what to do and what not to do. When we integrate how we treat and reward people with those decisions, we can create an innovative organization.

Here's what effectiveness means:

- Across the organization, we work on the right work at the right time.
- People across the organization collaborate to ship and support the product. As a whole organization, we fulfill a customer's needs.
- We don't just do what we've always done; we fill the pipeline of possibilities so we can continue to work on the right work at

the right time. We experiment and innovate at all levels of the organization. We enable change at all levels of the organization.

My experience leads me to say that when we manage for effectiveness *first*, we can then manage for efficiency. Russell Ackoff said, "The righter we do the wrong thing, the wronger we become. . . . Getting the right thing wrong is better than putting the wrong thing right."[1]

Some of our traditional management practices create inefficiencies. Here are some common inefficiencies. I address each of these examples in a future chapter:

- Ask people to multitask in the name of utilization.
- Create processes where the cost of the tracking outweighs the savings we might get from the tracking. I've seen organizations that ask technical people to track their time in 15-minute increments. Or to itemize every expense on a business trip—even the water that the person might buy at the airport.
- Demand that people use a centralized approach to purchasing office supplies, travel, or anything else that requires customized information.

We only *appear* to use economies of scale when we do these things in knowledge work. In reality, we create bureaucracy, which makes the work that much more difficult.

TIP In general, when we attempt to use economies of scale for knowledge workers, we create more inefficiencies.

We have alternatives to manage our funding and our cash flow—and to make sure we can trust people to deliver necessary outcomes *and* manage the money.

When we're effective, we optimize for *organizational* throughput. You might measure the change in customers and revenue—not just the number of projects or features you release.

---

[1] https://thesystemsthinker.com/transforming-the-systems-movement/

If you ever measure a system with a single-dimension output measurement, such as the number of releases, people optimize for that single measure.

Years ago, I performed an assessment where the managers created antagonistic incentives between developers and testers. The developers received bonuses based on meeting their (dictated) milestones. The testers received bonuses when they reported more defects than their quota.

Both sets of people gamed the system. The developers "met" every single date by not finishing the code. They checked in unfinished work.

If a tester found a problem in one language, the tester could check the other six languages and report an additional six issues.

Both developers and testers suffered from single-output measurement evaluations. No one checked the desired outcomes: did the product work so the customers would buy it and use it?

When you evaluate people on *outputs*, they game the system—they optimize to create those outputs.

When you evaluate *outcomes*, you get products that work. You get excellent customer support. You get an organization that works in harmony for the good of the entire organization. And, you can't get outcomes unless people work together in cross-functional teams in flow efficiency. That flow efficiency thinking includes the managers.

Evaluating effectiveness is more complicated than it sounds. The first piece of effectiveness is creating an environment that helps people succeed.

The environment shapes everyone's behavior—including yours.

1.4 Environment Shapes Everyone's Behavior

You may have heard the famous quote popularly attributed to Peter Drucker:

"Culture eats strategy for breakfast."

When Drucker said that, he meant that the culture you create and reinforce matters more than any strategy you create. Table 1 has some examples of the differences between what people say and the reality of the culture.

Desired Culture vs Reality of the Culture	
Stated Strategy or Culture (We say we want this)	The Organization's Reality (Reality of how we treat each other, decide what we discuss, and what we reward.)
We want collaborative work.	We measure individuals.
We want you to be entreprenurial.	You have no time to learn or experiment.
We want faster throughput.	You multitask on several products and projects.
We want to see working product so we know you're working faster and cheaper.	You must estimate and provide Gantt charts (or other predictive measures).
You have autonomy.	We plan the details of the products and projects.
We encourage change.	Plan the work and work the plan.
Quality matters.	Just get it out.

Table 1: Desired Culture vs. the Reality

Does it matter if what managers say doesn't match their actions? Yes, and not just for our integrity. It matters because the environment—where what people say differs from their actions—shapes everyone's behaviors.

Kurt Lewin, a psychologist, published his equation in *Principles of Topological Psychology* back in 1936. His equation says that the behavior of a person (B) is a function of the person (P) and the environment (E):

$$B = f(P, E)$$

As people, P, we perceive the environment, E. We act in ways that make sense to us. Those actions comprise our behavior (B).

Here's an example I see too often. Managers want the benefit of an agile or lean approach to software, which means they expect people to collaborate. At the same time, they tell people they have unique, personal objectives. People won't get raises or bonuses unless they fulfill those personal objectives.

What would you do? What many of us do. We choose ways to fulfill the personal objectives, so we don't miss out on *our* raise or *our* bonus.

You can *tell* people over and over that you want collaboration. You won't get sustained collaboration until you remove personal rewards. That goes for managers, too.

Think back to the last time you saw someone "not perform". Could their "lack" of performance be a reasonable response to the environment?

We all bring our unique personality, experience, and beliefs to our work. Our differences can help us create great products. The more managers realize the environment shapes people's behaviors, the more managers will pay attention to that environment.

Ask these questions about your environment:

- Are you able to decriminalize mistakes? Do you encourage risk-taking and learning from mistakes?
- Can you support experiments?
- How many problems can teams, groups, and collaborative people solve on their own?

The environment managers and leaders create can encourage or block innovation.

1.5 Encourage Management Flow Efficiency

For too long, we've asked managers to work in silos. We've judged managers by "their" performance or the performance of "their" teams or groups. That's resource efficiency. (For more information about resource efficiency and flow efficiency, see *This is Lean: Resolving the Efficiency Paradox* [MOA13] or *The Principles of Product Development Flow: Second Generation Lean Product Development*

[REI09]. I also wrote about the problems of resource efficiency thinking in Book 2.)

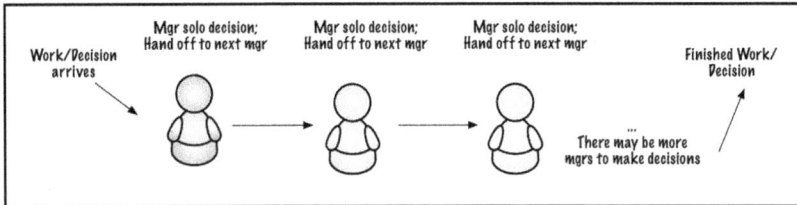

Figure 1.1: Management Resource Efficiency

The manager assigns work or decides for that manager's team or group. After that decision, the manager hands off work to the next manager. Managers incur tremendous delays between the various decisions.

When managers focus on *their* functional group, we create hierarchies like the one in Figure 1.2.

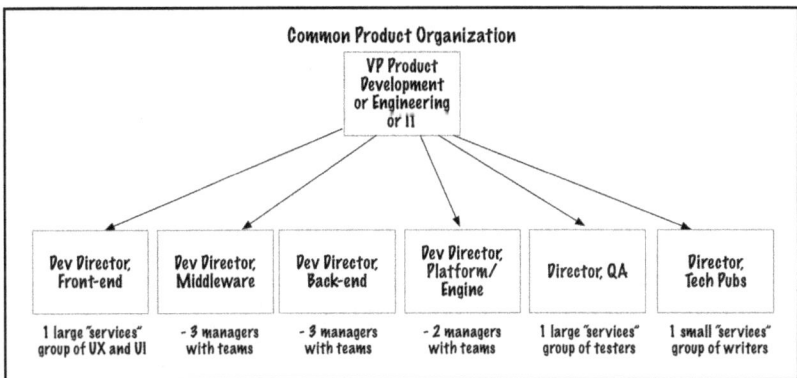

Figure 1.2: Common Product Development Organization

In silos, such as these, each manager focuses on his or her team's functional expertise. Managers tend to focus on *their* issues, not issues across the organization. And, managers tend to think in resource efficiency, optimizing down for each person's work—not across for an overarching organizational goal.

When we think in hierarchies, we assume the *information* flows up and down the hierarchy. Here's how hierarchical communication flows up and down.

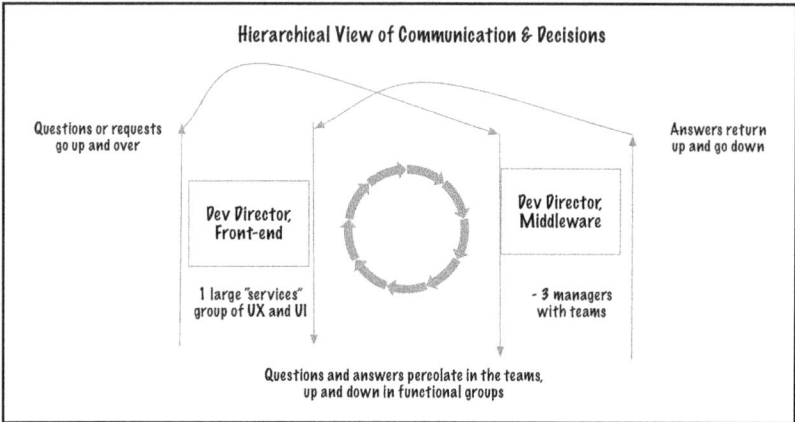

Figure 1.3: How we think information moves in a hierarchy

We assume that when teams have questions, they ask their manager. That manager then asks a colleague. The second manager might decide or ask the teams to decide. Then, the new information goes back up the hierarchy and down to the team with the questions.

When we reinforce a hierarchy, we reinforce the idea that managers make most of these decisions. Many organizations reward managers for those decisions.

However, that's not how people work effectively in organizations.

People create relationships across the organization in unpredictable ways. Sometimes, they connect via shared interests in the work or something outside of work.

If you graph the way people communicate and work in an organization, you see a small-world network of seemingly random connections, as in Figure 1.4 on page 15. (See *Here Comes Everybody: The Power of Organizing with Organizations* [SHI08] for more information about these networks.)

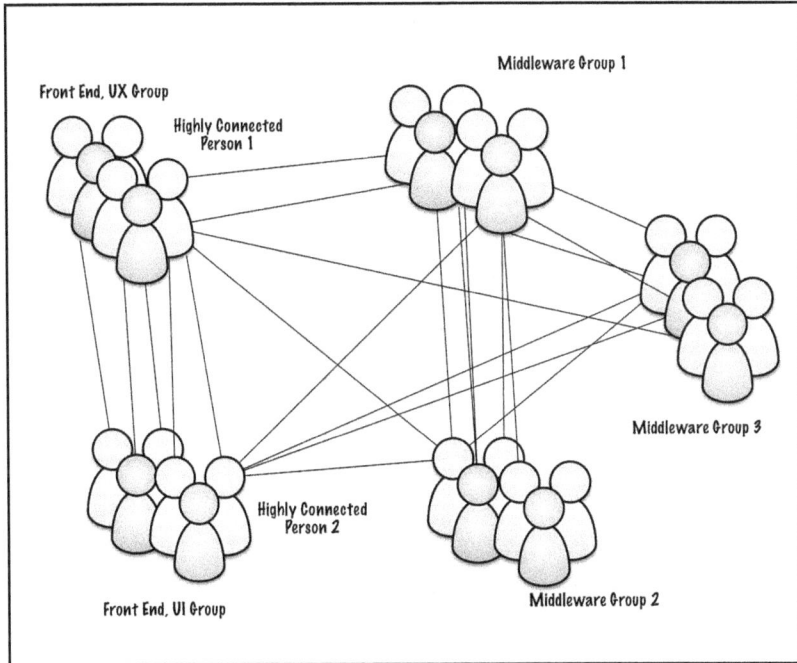

Figure 1.4: Small-World Network

Some people connect with more people. I call them Highly Connected so you can see that their connections matter. Some people only connect with people in their teams or groups. That turns out to be okay, too—as long as the managers create an environment where small-world networks thrive.

I created single-function teams in Figure 1.4, because most organizations still create single-function teams and then matrix people into projects.

Effective managers work across the organization—at every level. They use flow efficiency to create management teams, as in Figure 1.5 on page 16.

When management teams work in flow, they create teams at their level to surface and resolve cross-organizational issues and

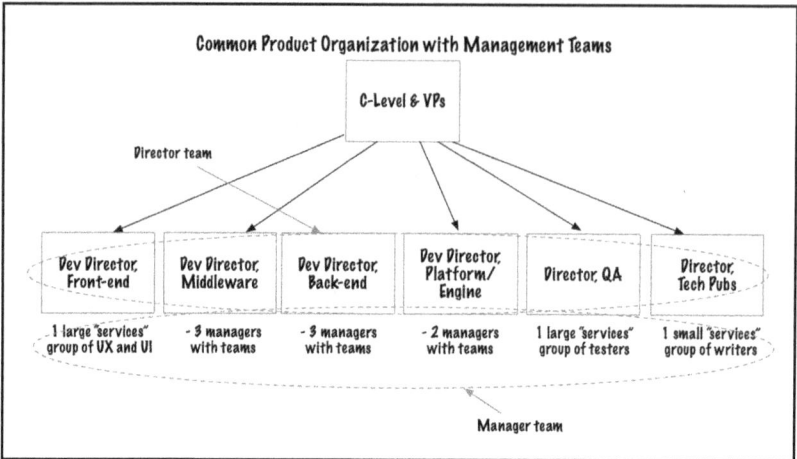

Figure 1.5: Flow-Based Management Teams

challenges. The managers collaborate on the project portfolio so they all agree on the organization's purpose and work towards that purpose.

Notice that you don't have to change your organization to use management teams who work more in flow.

However, if you decide you want to work in flow efficiency as management teams, you might find the organizational structure in Figure 1.6 works better for you.

The directors and the managers also act as cross-functional teams as in Figure 1.5. In Figure 1.6 on page 17, the managers do not focus on the *content* of the teams. The managers learn enough to serve cross-functional teams, not a single-function team.

In Figure 1.6, I showed arrows only going "down" from the more senior managers to the less senior managers. The information flows both ways. However the managers serve the people and teams farther down on the chart. Yes, I'm using hierarchical terms to describe a flatter organization. I want to make sure people who are accustomed to hierarchy can understand these ideas.

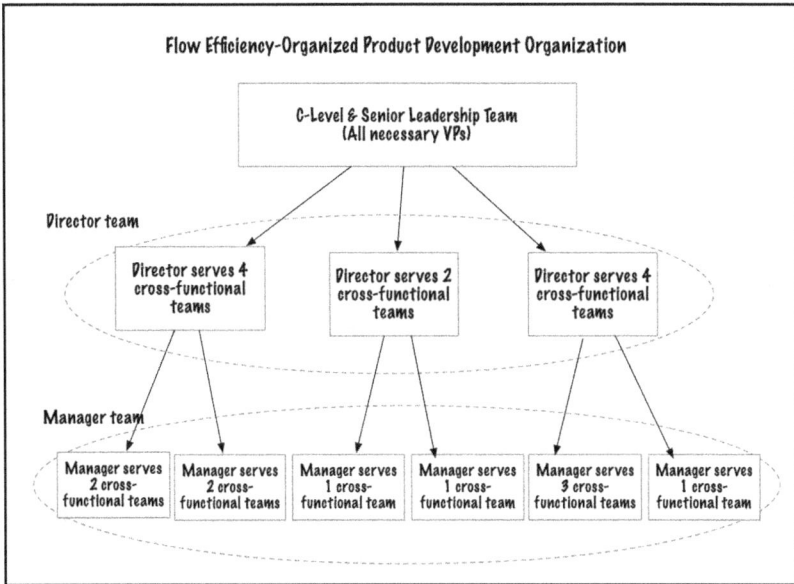

Figure 1.6: Flow Efficiency-Organized Product Development Organization

When I've worked with flow-efficiency management teams, we discover that managers can serve more teams because they're not involved in the day-to-day work of the team. There is no set number of teams a manager can serve. That number depends—at minimum—on how well the team can manage itself. (I'm not saying this is easy. I'll talk more about this later in Increase Management Capability on page 27.)

You might think if you change the org chart, you can change how people act. You don't have to change the org chart first. Instead, consider these principles of management flow:

- Managers change their focus from "down" to the team to "up" to the product, service, or organization. That's why defining the "why" helps the team focus on the outcomes.
- Middle managers collaborate across the organization to create a balanced project portfolio. They see where teams or

team members might need training opportunities. They see opportunities for process and product innovation.

- Senior managers collaborate to create a coherent set of products that customers will buy. They refine the culture with their choices of what to reward.

I first wrote about flow efficiency for teams in Book 2. The quick explanation is that every outcome is a function of the work time and the wait time.

To see your flow efficiency percentage, add all the work time and divide by the wait time. For example, if managers meet one hour a week over three weeks to decide, that's three hours of work time plus 504 hours of wait time (168 hours per week times three weeks), for a total of 507 hours to make the decision. The flow efficiency is 3 hours divided by 507 hours, .0059, multiplied by 100 to get the percentage. This percentage is .59.

Let me say that again without the numbers. The management work time is only three hours. However, because it took three *weeks* to decide, the managers had very little efficiency.

Just imagine if the managers had spent three hours over the course of one day to make their decision. The work time is three hours. Let's assume the managers started at 9 A.M. and decided at 5 P.M. Three hours of work time plus 5 hours of wait time gives you a flow efficiency of 3 divided by 8, a percentage of 37.5.

If you extend flow efficiency to managers, you'll gain more throughput than you can imagine. That's because the managers collaborate for the good of the organization, not their self-interest.

When managers collaborate, they can create more congruence across the organization.

1.6 Create a Congruent Organization

In Book 1, I discussed personal congruence and the balance a manager needs to manage him or herself. In Book 2, I discussed how to apply

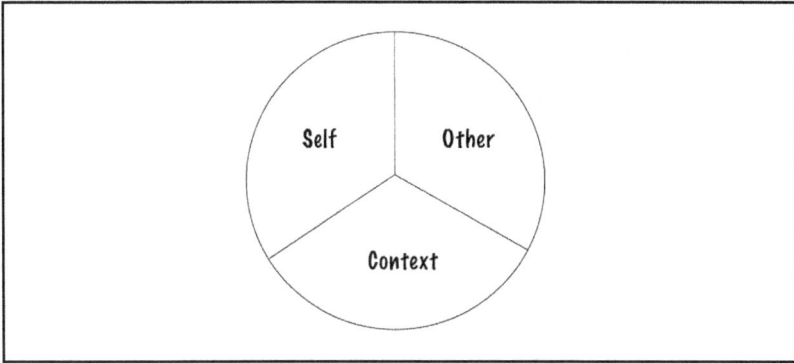

Figure 1.7: Satir Congruence Model

congruence to how people work with each other. In this book, it's about how to have a congruent organization.

The brief explanation of congruence:

- When we ignore the other person's needs, we blame them.
- When we ignore our needs, we placate the other person.
- When we ignore the needs of both ourselves and the others, we are super-reasonable, not acknowledging we are human.
- When we ignore the context, we're irrelevant.

When we balance all three—our needs, the other person, and the context—we are congruent.

Here are some examples of congruent behaviors in organizations:

- When managers say, "People are our most important asset," they create time for training and learning. The managers create learning time for people and teams.
- When managers decide what to do first, second, third, and never, and then they stick to it for long enough for the teams to deliver something useful. That way, no one multitasks, and the entire organization succeeds.
- When managers eliminate individual goals and focus on how to create goals that elevate the whole organization.

These actions balance the needs of each person, the customer, and the entire organization.

You've seen plenty of incongruent behaviors:

- When the company decides to reimburse travel expenses more than a week after the travel so the company can use the float.
- When managers say, "Do more with less." That statement has no meaning.
- When people have no flexibility for office organization, office furnishings, or the career ladder. For example, your ability to get a desk or a chair depends on your salary level. Or, the people or team can't experiment with various project approaches. Or, HR decides that no one can be eligible for a raise except at one specific time each year.

Why blame people for being human?

1.7 Create Integrity in the Organization

When you think about integrity in the organization, what do you consider? The values I discussed in the previous books still hold:

- Transparency. Can you share enough about how the organization progresses so people can see how they fit into the organization?
- Fairness. You don't have to treat people exactly the same way, as long as people feel they have fair treatment.
- Consistency. When you're consistent with the (hopefully few) policies, people know what to expect.
- Avoiding blame. At the organizational level, do you encourage collaboration and mistake-proofing so that people can avoid problems?
- Build respect into all interactions. Make it easy to recognize people and update their pay without having to wait for another salary year.

I'm writing this in the era of COVID-19 amid discussions about how and when people should return to work. One more part of integrity is physical and psychological safety. If people don't feel safe, in either dimension, they won't want to return to work. Leaders who don't create both a physically and psychologically safe environment lack integrity.

If you think you can't afford to keep people safe, why would you ask them to come to work? Or, would you put yourself in their shoes and do their job to see how to make the work safe?

The more you exercise your integrity, the easier it is to create an entire organization built on respect and integrity.

And, the more innovation you want, the more the managers optimize for the effectiveness of *outcomes*. The managers leave efficiency issues to the teams.

Management flow efficiency helps everyone manage for outcomes, not outputs. The more the managers work in flow, the easier it is to manage *for* change.

1.8 Manage for Change and Innovation

When we manage for innovation, we act differently than when we operate for our self-interest or the short-term.

We work as collaborative management teams at every level. We encourage collaboration and flow efficiency, not just in technical teams, but in management teams.

And, we are more able to balance the immediate needs for cashflow with building for the future.

As you read this book, I'll ask you to experiment.

I'm not asking you to change your beliefs. Your beliefs arise from the results of your actions and interactions with others. Change your behaviors as an experiment. Then, you can decide if you want to change your beliefs and the culture.

You don't need to be perfect. If you can explain when you experiment, people will build empathy, trust, and respect with you.

CHAPTER 2

Does Management Require Practice?

When you look at managers from the outside, their work might not seem that difficult. Go to some meetings, and talk with people all day. What's the big deal?

Managers solve problems the teams can't solve. Managers address the questions of which customers to serve and when. Managers decide on the strategy, which defines the mix of products and services. Managers decide about finances and cash flow.

The way the managers discuss and decide reflects the organizational culture.

With any luck, the managers work together, as a cohort, to optimize for the organization, not any one of the managers. When managers work across the organization, they learn from each other and create management flow.

Very few people outside those meetings have visibility into how managers treat each other or those conversations. And, the effect of those conversations? To create the environment in which everyone can do their best work.

The best managers learn by practicing and from feedback. They practice. Even if no one can see the practice.

2.1 Myth: Management Doesn't Need Practice

Sheryl, a director, sat in the division's strategy meeting. Their product had been a great success until last week. That's when their major competitor had released a brand new product that changed the entire market. Combined with the seasonal sales decrease, they needed new ideas now.

Sheryl had never faced an emergency like this before. She was glad she was able to work with her colleagues.

She was worried about leaving her department's managers alone. Normally, she checked in with them when she walked around. However, that wasn't possible this week.

The managers knew where to take the product—that wasn't a problem. But, not everyone had a ton of management practice. Especially Terry. She'd promoted him just last month. On the one hand, his instincts were often right. On the other hand, he didn't have a lot of management experience.

She used her phone to make a note to remind the managers to support each other. Sheryl turned off her phone and hoped her team had learned how to collaborate to support each other. She'd have to address that later.

She needed to focus on this strategy emergency. This product problem might be the end of the company's viability. That was more important right now than her managers' abilities.

In the meantime, Terry was confused about a problem. He decided to ask Johnny for help. Terry leaned his head in and knocked on the door. "Got a minute to talk through a problem I have?"

Johnny nodded. "Yup, let me save what I'm doing."

Terry walked in and sat down at Johnny's visitor table and pulled up a diagram on his tablet.

Johnny walked over and sat down across from Terry. "What's up?"

Terry took a deep breath. "First, I don't get what Sheryl's been doing. She's been in meetings the last week. She's only come out for *our* one-on-ones. I've been trying to catch her. I wanted to ask her some questions about how to give feedback to Cathy about this problem." Terry shook his head. "I thought I'd ask you for help."

"Good idea," Johnny said.

Terry pointed to his architecture picture. "I know this architecture is not going to work. I need to find the right words for the feedback. I thought management would be so easy. When Sheryl asked me if I wanted to be a manager, I thought this part would be a piece of cake—but it's not. Every time I think of what I want to say, it comes out wrong."

Johnny nodded. "Yup, I have the same problem with some of the senior people in my teams, too."

Terry continued. "Every time I text Sheryl asking for a little time, she asks if it's an emergency. I say no, and she asks if we can wait for our one-on-one. I say okay. She's not normally like this. What's going on? Do you know?"

Johnny said, "You know the new product our competitor released last week?"

Terry nodded.

"I think all the product people and our division managers are trying to figure out what to do. We're in the slow season, and they don't want that product to cause our death spiral."

"Oh, got it," Terry said. "I was so focused on my work, I didn't even think about what she was doing. She always makes management look so easy."

Johnny grinned. "Yeah, she does. Even now, in uncertainty, she still responds, at least a little."

Terry thought for a minute. "Do you think she needs help, even if it's a stupid thing to ask?"

Johnny leaned back in his chair. "Gee, I never thought of that. Maybe she does. We could text her and see if she does need help. She might appreciate it. At least she would know that we're thinking of her."

Terry nodded.

"In the meantime," Johnny said, "want to discuss what you're going to say to Cathy about her design? Maybe you shouldn't be the one to say it. You're the manager, but you're not the be-all and end-all for design decisions, right? How does the rest of the team feel about it? Can you enlist someone else?"

Terry nodded. "Oh, maybe that's a better way to offer her feedback," he said. "I don't have to be the one to tell her that her design isn't going to work. She hates it when I tell her these things anyway. Now that I'm in management, she doesn't want to hear that from me."

Johnny grinned and said, "Well, maybe you don't know enough anymore to tell her that. Maybe that's why she doesn't want to hear it from you. You need to have other people tell her—especially if it's true. Why do you think her design isn't good enough?"

Terry pointed to the picture on his tablet. "See this over here? Well, this is going to fail in these three ways under load in these circumstances." Terry and Johnny discussed the technical details for a few minutes.

"Okay, you convinced me," Johnny said. "You know, I just thought of something from back when I was a developer and I wanted to get people to think about their designs."

Terry cocked his head to the right. "Oh?"

Johnny nodded. "I asked everyone to choose someone else's design and say, 'Generate three ways this design will solve problems for us. And, think about three ways your design will fail.' Have you tried that approach?"

Terry shook his head. "Nope. That's about the Rule of Three, right?"

Johnny nodded. "Yup. My experience says if you can't think of three positives and three negatives, you haven't thought clearly enough about the problem, and we all need to go back to the drawing board and experiment some more. Maybe even try a short timeboxed experiment to get more ideas. Maybe an hour or two total."

"Nice," Terry said.

"That way, you don't need to give Cathy specific feedback about her idea, but you can get everybody to give her feedback, or get her to think about her idea some more. And, we can give Sheryl the breathing room she needs for her summit. Okay?" Johnny asked.

"Great idea!" Terry said. "You have this management thing knocked, don't you?"

"Uh, not really," Johnny replied. "I've been working at it a lot longer than you. It's still hard work, and I need practice to manage right. Well, at least, not too wrong. Let's bring in the rest of our management team and see what we can do for Sheryl."

Terry nodded. "Good idea."

2.2 Increase Management Capability

All three of these managers knew they needed to increase their management capabilities.

- Sheryl needed to learn how to manage strategic product problems.
- Terry needed to learn how to offer feedback to a senior person on his team.
- Johnny practiced how to coach a peer.

Managers aren't born knowing how to do these things. Managers need to increase their management capabilities.

When managers collaborate, they create a learning cohort, a symmathesy. (See *Symmathesy: A Word in Progress* [BAT15] for why we are a product of our learning cohort.)

When managers work together, they often model management flow efficiency. And, they help each other create more management capability.

Johnny and Terry learned together. Together, they helped Terry discover a way to manage Terry's feedback problem:

1. Let other people offer feedback.
2. Verify that the problem exists.
3. Use a problem-solving technique: Find three great things about someone else's design and three problems in your own design. (This approach comes from *Manage It! Your Guide to Modern, Pragmatic Project Management* [ROT07].)

4. Experiment more: Create short timeboxed experiments to develop alternative solutions.

Terry and Johnny discussed the Rule of Three: One solution is a trap, two solutions is a dilemma, and three possibilities breaks logjam thinking, helping people think of more possibilities. (See *Behind Closed Doors: Secrets of Great Management* [BCD05] for this and other management approaches.)

Terry and Johnny modeled several principles from Consider These Innovation Leadership Principles (page 1):

- Empathy with each other, their team members, and their manager.
- Created a safe and collaborative environment in which people can discuss, explore, and learn.
- Broadened the problem-solving perspective to the entire team, instead of only Terry's perspective.

In parallel, Terry and Johnny—and their colleagues—can offer Sheryl help and support for the product problem. Only Sheryl knows when she will be ready for their help and support.

2.3 Create Your Management Cohort

Even when people have great instincts, they need coaching and practice to become great managers. Lencioni in *The Four Obsessions of an Extraordinary Executive* [LEN00] explains this for executive teams. All management teams need to learn together.

When the leader asks the managers to work as a cohort, collaborating, the managers can learn faster together. They might coach each other, as Terry and Johnny did here.

However, when managers learn as a cohort, the entire department or division works better. The managers work in flow efficiency, integrating speed and integrity into their decisions.

Here are some possibilities to create your management cohort:

- Ask for coaching from your peers. When you ask for help or support, you're exhibiting strength, not weakness. (I wrote more about this in Book 1.)
- Generate a list of topics you'd like to learn more about, and learn with your colleagues.
- Explain the idea of a cohort or symmathesy to everyone: your peers and your manager.
- Look for a recent time your department's management decision-making process would have benefited from everyone working on the same problem at the same time.

I have not yet met a "natural" manager. I have met many people who used the growth mindset (Carol Dweck's *Mindset: The New Psychology of Success* [DWE07]) to practice parts of their management role.

The growth mindset rejects the idea that skills are inborn talents. Instead, we can learn, practice new skills, and persist to master these skills. We learn from feedback. And, if we fail, we can learn from our mistakes.

The more you practice, the more management capabilities you will gain. Your management might look easy, and that's because you practice.

2.4 Options to Practice Management

Consider these options to learn and practice your management skills:

1. Create your management cohort, even if your manager doesn't specifically encourage you to do so.
2. Ask for coaching from your colleagues. I had to ask specifically around the Rule of Three. I had to practice to move past the first obvious alternative.
3. Practice your coaching with other managers, to obtain feedback in a safe environment.

4. Ask your manager for feedback about your management skills. I found that I needed to improve my interpersonal skills and my "poker face" skills. I still don't have much of a poker face—my reactions show on my face. I often have to say, "I'm frustrated with the situation, not you. I value the fact you brought me this information."

5. Manage up, especially using your influence to manage your manager.

When I incorporated deliberate practice as a manager, I became a better manager.

CHAPTER 3

Should We Treat Everyone the Same Way?

Too many managers and HR people believe we must treat everyone the same way to be fair. That thinking assumes everyone brainstorms the same way, that everyone likes the same kind of work, and that everyone has the same goals for their career.

Not true.

Everyone has different goals for their career. Those goals often change throughout a person's life and career.

Early in my career, I wanted to learn and practice a wide variety of technical skills. I also wanted to take an additional week of vacation.

After I had children, I wanted to bound the start and end of my workdays so I could manage the challenges of having small children. As the children grew, I wanted time to go to their school performances. I didn't need that flexibility until I had children.

And, I didn't want to create resentment in the team for my "special" treatment. I broached the topic with my team, not just my manager. I explained when I needed extra time and what I was willing to do for the team to make that happen.

People want fair *treatment*—they don't need or expect precisely the same things from the company. They know people aren't equivalent.

3.1 Myth: We Must Treat Everyone the Same Way

Two weeks ago, Susan, a manager, asked Karen, a senior developer, what she wanted for the next step in her career development plan.

"Hi, Karen. Have you thought about your career development plan?"

"Yes, I have. First, I want to modify my book allowance a little. Instead of just a book allowance for me, I want you to extend the allowance to the entire team. I was reading about a new way to do a reading group, and I think it will work this time. Last time, I couldn't get anyone to read with me."

Susan nodded.

"I have an idea about how to encourage people to read in time. Instead of just reading a chapter a week, I have exercises and games for each chapter. I want to do those instead of just discussions. I think that will work. And, since I'm working on my facilitation skills, that will play really nicely into developing those skills."

"What a great idea!" Susan agreed. "How much money do you think you need for the first month? We can assess how things have gone after the group has read the first book and you've developed the first set of exercises."

"I might need to go to a local conference, too," Karen said. "And, I want to go to that national conference in November."

"Okay," Susan said. "Now that I have the whole plan, I can add the expenses and see what I can shake loose. Give me a couple of days, and I'll let you know."

Later that day, Susan met with David, another senior developer. He strolled into Susan's office and sat down. He grinned his deceptively lazy grin.

"Susan, what's shakin'?"

"Dave, I'm supposed to ask you that! Tell me, have you thought about your career development plan?"

"I have, and I have a little problem. I don't want to go anywhere for training. I just want to stay here and work, and drive the kids and do that soccer-dad thing. I like the fact I get to leave early a couple of days a week and coach Little League for Little-Dave and take Jenny and Barbara to gymnastics and dance. I would never have pegged myself for the minivan-dad kind of guy, but I'm loving it. The kids say so much when I'm driving them. In a couple of years, Jenny will be able to drive, but until then, I don't want to travel."

Susan smiled. "I suspect that's not a problem; I bet you don't have to go anywhere. What makes you think that's a problem?"

"Well, I need to work on my people skills. I'm fine here in the team—I can pair with anyone, I can interview anyone technical—but whenever I want to find out what's going on with the stories from sales to get a better idea of what they want for the acceptance criteria, I ask them questions. They look at me as if I'm from outer space. I'm not sure Sales and I speak the same language."

"Is it just you, or do other people have the same problem? Should I look into bringing in training?"

"I don't know," Dave said. "I'll have to check with other people." He made some notes in his notebook.

"I'll gather some data, too," Susan said. "What else did you want to work on?"

"Well, this is going to sound a little strange, but I want to start a more formal lunch-and-learn series about the guts of our system. The system is getting bigger. We've been hiring more people—we're up to three teams now," Dave said.

Susan nodded.

Dave continued. "We're managing our technical decisions and avoiding cruft. I want to make sure we keep making good decisions. So I want to make sure everyone understands what's going on. I want everyone to stay synched with each other: all the testers and all the developers. I don't know if this is career development for me or for everyone else, but I see a need, and I want to make sure it happens."

Susan nodded. "Dave, that's not strange—that's a great idea. How often will it be? And, are you sure you want to impose learning at lunch? What about a weekly specific time instead of lunch? I'm happy to offer healthy snacks."

"Oh," Dave said. "I thought you wouldn't want us to take time away from the product work."

"This *is* the product work," Susan said with a grin. "You'll take responsibility for the series? And get the people and help them craft their talks? That's a lot of work."

Dave grinned. "I'd like to start biweekly—once every two weeks. I like the idea of drinks and healthy snacks." He laughed out loud. "When I gain weight, my wife isn't happy. When she's not happy, no one is happy."

Susan laughed.

He paused and thought. "I'll do the first talk so people can see how we might learn together. Then I'll let people know I want more talks and I'll line up more speakers. You want to be a speaker?"

"Sure, but what do you want me to talk about?"

Dave smiled and then got serious. "How our agile approaches allow us to make promises to our clients that we couldn't otherwise. How the roadmap and the backlog allow us to see business value and stop doing work that doesn't matter. Some of the younger guys don't know we used to work differently and that we have a real business advantage now."

Susan agreed, and Dave left.

A few minutes later, Brian arrived. Brian is a tester in his early 20s. He's new to the organization, and no manager has ever asked him to define his career development plan before. He plopped down in Susan's visitor chair. Then his right leg started to jump up and down a hundred times a minute.

"Hi, Susan. I think I did what you want. I'm a little confused."

"Well, that's why we talk about it. What do you want to learn about?"

"Well, I want to learn more about the system, that's for sure. I don't think I know nearly enough. And, I've been pair testing with Dale and Liza. I'd like to know more about the database, so I think I'd like to pair test with Michelle, our DBA, or even have her train me in DBA-ness, if that's even a word."

"It's enough of a word for me. Have you asked Michelle?"

"I can do that?" Brian seemed surprised.

"You don't have to wait for my permission," Susan said. "You're on the team with her. If she picks up a story, you say something like, 'I'd like to work on that with you.' And if she says no, and no one on the team helps you, then ask me, and I'll show you how to help her say yes. But she will most likely say yes the first time."

"Oh, I didn't realize that. Okay, I'll talk to Michelle at lunch and tell her I want to work with her."

Brian's leg was still going a mile a minute. Susan waited a few seconds and asked, "Brian, is there something else you want to ask me?"

"Um, yes. It's not really about career development, but I don't know when the right time is."

"Well, ask away."

"I want to take a big bicycling trip this summer, four weeks worth. That's not career development, that's sort of personal development. I don't care if I take two weeks without pay or something like that. But I don't know when to ask. Is that possible?" Brian's leg was threatening lift-off from his body.

"Sure, it is. I'm delighted you told me now so that we can plan for that much time off." Susan smiled, and Brian's leg stopped.

Susan had similar conversations with the same structure with each person she serves. She couldn't say "yes" to all their requests. However, Susan has learned that knowing what people want helps her plan for the future.

She treats people fairly, not equally. That's because each person is unique. But in one way, she does treat each person the same—with respect.

3.2 Everyone Wants Something Different

What makes one person happy might make another person miserable. Most people want a challenging job—a job with autonomy and ways to learn. Susan's team members make their own decisions about their career development. Susan facilitates their decisions and obtains the funds—she does not decide for the individual. How could she? She doesn't know what each person wants or needs. Susan is not a mind reader.

People want a fair working environment. They want regular feedback about their performance, meaning when they do something good or not so good. They don't want feedback once a year—that's too late.

When people are ready for more responsibility, they want these things:

- To stop work that no longer challenges them.
- To start work that does challenge them *and*
- That aligns the "why" for the business and for the person.

Some people discover that they need help in creating acceptance criteria for stories. Some people want to experiment with facilitation. And, some people want to pair with a specific person to learn from that person.

People want and deserve meaningful work for fair treatment. In return, they will offer the best job they can do.

That's what people want from work.

You can't provide that if you treat people equally because people are not equal. We are unique individuals.

As long as we have to treat people equally, we will end up with unequal situations. As long as we treat people fairly, we will end up with a fair workplace. And that creates a wonderful place in which to work.

Don't try to treat each person in precisely the same way. Be transparent and tell people you will treat them fairly.

3.3 **Options for Fair Treatment**

As you think about what people want, don't guess. Ask them. You might not be able to offer them precisely what they want. But, you might.

1. Make sure you conduct one-on-ones with everyone at least once every two weeks. I like to review career goals at least once a month. (If you're not sure about one-on-ones, see Books 1 and 2.)

2. Write down what fair treatment looks like for each person you serve. I write this down in the file with my one-on-one notes.

3. As a management cohort (your colleagues and your manager), discuss what fair treatment looks like across the department. Ask your manager to continue that discussion up the organization. (Start with fair treatment in a team, then up to the department, then up to the division, etc.)

4. Decide whether you need to involve HR or whether all of you, as a management cohort, can create fair treatment for everyone in your part of the organization.

You can treat people fairly, and still allow for differences.

CHAPTER 4

Must We Manage Performance?

I "participated" in performance management in my very first job. My boss and I sat down and dutifully created my yearly goals. At our weekly one-on-ones, he offered me feedback and supported my work.

At the end of the year, I eagerly awaited my performance evaluation. I'd accomplished a lot.

I received an outstanding performance evaluation and a 15% raise—quite significant at the time.

I had lunch with some of my colleagues, and we compared the percentages of our raises. (You think people don't talk about money? Of course, they do.)

A male colleague congratulated me on my percentage. It was four percent higher than his. Then he told me how much he was making per year.

His salary was almost 10% higher than mine. And, that was after my monstrous raise.

I was angry. I made an appointment to see my manager after lunch. I told him what I learned, that a male colleague made more money than I did. Was I correct?

He nodded. I was.

I told him I wanted total pay parity now. I was willing to wait for the next paycheck. But I didn't want to wait another year for pay parity.

His exact words to me were, "I can't do that. I maxed out your raise. We offered the male college grads more than we offered the female grads last year."

I was stunned. "Even though I had relevant coursework and paid experience while I was in school? And, even after I've done a demonstrably better job?"

"Yes."

I learned something valuable. My evaluation was not about *my* performance. At least at that organization—and I suspect at many others—performance "management" is salary management. Performance "management" allows the organization to manage salary costs, not performance.

My boss had a too-small pool of salary increases. Even though I had exceeded all my goals and expectations, he could not compensate me fairly because the salary increases were not tied only to *my* performance. I *competed* with my colleagues for my salary increase.

And, because the "performance management" was really about salary management, the entire activity *looked* fair. (See Should We Treat Everyone the Same Way? on page 31.) However, none of us received appropriate salary treatment.

We had massive salary disparity.

That's because the company calculated increases based on our starting salary—not market value—and we competed for a too-small pool of salary increases. This organization created sexist hiring practices—both incongruent and lacking in integrity.

Many companies calculate your salary increase based on your current salary plus whatever the manager thinks you accomplished in the past year.

That means that people who don't negotiate—or don't know how to or don't realize they *should* negotiate—receive a lower salary (and bonus). (If you suffer from low self-esteem, you tend not to negotiate. You're grateful anyone offers you a job. Sheryl Sandberg discusses how women tend to feel this way more often than men in *Lean In: Women, Work, and the Will to Lead* [SAN13].)

From what I've seen, if you take a lower salary at an early job, that lower salary might persist throughout your career—especially if you stay at that early job for many years. And, while your company might not discriminate based on gender as mine did, you can be sure the company discriminates on something.

Salary Transparency Can Solve Salary Disparity

Salary disparity exists because the salaries are secret. No one knows what other people earn.

The more secrecy, the more disparity can occur. If companies published everyone's salary, everyone could assess their situation relative to the rest of the organization.

I know of very few organizations that publish their salaries. However, transparent salaries make disparity impossible.

When the organization ties job performance to money and bases raises on current salary, they're not "managing" a person's performance. They're managing salary costs. And, that means managing performance can lead to employee *disengagement*. (I left that first job within six weeks of my conversation with my boss. Yes, I found a better job for more money—and better engagement.)

4.1 Myth: Performance Management Creates Employee Engagement

Becky, a senior engineer, was ready for her one-on-one. Three months ago, she and Stan, her boss, were supposed to design her yearly performance plan. She thought they were crazy to create an annual plan, but that's what HR wanted.

She wanted to limit the number of goals to four or maybe five. She was pretty sure Stan wanted at least a dozen. In the one-on-one, they compromised on eight goals, all project-based.

Two months ago, when Becky's projects changed, she told Stan she wanted to change her yearly goals. He postponed that discussion.

One month ago, Becky's projects changed again. She asked Stan to work with her to update her yearly goals. He postponed that conversation again.

Now, three months later, Becky's projects have changed again. Two days ago, she told Stan she wanted to address her yearly goals in her next one-on-one. She wasn't going to let him slither out of the discussion today.

Becky arrived in Stan's office with several documents. She waited until Stan joined her at his visitor's table.

"Stan, we need to revisit my yearly goals."

Stan frowned. "Why?"

"Because I'm not on any of the original eight projects. You canceled half of the projects. The other half you gave to other people. You've changed everything I'm supposed to do every month this year. I'm concerned you're going to tell me I'm not pushing myself enough for the raise I'll want."

Stan looked around his office and sighed.

"That was your plan, wasn't it?"

"Not really," he said. "But I have no idea how to give you the work you need for the promotion and the raise you want."

Becky leaned forward and whispered. "Make my goals about how I help other people improve."

He looked at her with a blank look. "Help other people, not projects?"

She resumed in a normal voice. "You know as well as I do that I'll change projects a gazillion more times this year. But focusing me on helping other people improve instead of my specific projects? That's performance management at the team level, not the individual."

Stan nodded. "Well, that makes a ton more sense than what we do now, especially since we want all of you to collaborate. I have to get approval."

Becky stood. "Get it, Stan. I'm not spending another week here if you don't."

"Are you threatening to quit?" he asked.

"I'm promising," Becky said. "I've been here for more than three years. Every year, we've changed my goals several times a year. This year, it's been every month."

Stan nodded. "That's true," he said.

"Individual goals don't make sense and don't work," Becky said. "You don't manage my performance. I do. You know that, too. Especially since we've started to use agile approaches, individual performance management makes no sense."

Stan leaned back. "Well, that's true." he paused. "Aren't you going to sit down for the rest of our one-on-one?"

"Nope. We don't need any more one-on-ones," she said.

Stan raised both his eyebrows. "Oh?" he asked.

"Look," Becky said, "You have two big action items. You need to work with HR to end this top-down performance management. And, while you're at it, make sure you start to create some form of team-based compensation if you want us to work as an engaged team."

She left.

Stan slumped in his chair. Performance management was a huge problem now.

4.2 Performance Management Creates Disengagement

I've asked both managers and technical people about any positive experiences with performance management. Many people find the feedback helpful. Most people—including the managers—do not find goal setting or the yearly need for paperwork useful to create employee engagement or to accomplish the work.

I addressed the issue of performance reviews from the employee's perspective in Book 2. This chapter is about the organizational aspect of why performance management creates employee *disengagement.*

Here's why performance management creates disengagement and discourages innovation:

- In a knowledge work organization, we want people to learn with and from their peers at every level. And, we want people to learn with and from their managers. In performance management, the learning flows from the *manager* "down" to the employee (the person who does the work). The employee does not help the manager learn—even though the employee knows the most about their work.
- In an innovative organization, the basis for performance changes during the year. The goals we so carefully craft at the start of the year become useless within weeks or months. The organization changes the mix of work.
- Performance management focuses on an individual's resource efficiency, not a team's effectiveness. Or several teams' effectiveness if we want to deliver a large effort. If we want people to change their behavior, we need to change the environment. (See Environment Shapes Everyone's Behavior on page 10.)

Many aspects of performance management create disengagement. The worst example I've seen is ranking people in the organization.

4.3 Ranking People Creates Disengagement

Have you ever been part of an organization that attempts to rank each person in a department and then fire the bottom x%, where x was often 10%? Jack Welch of GE publicized and used this strategy. (His nickname was "Neutron Jack.")

If you force rank—even once—the people who find this practice disrespectful will leave the organization. I did.

You successfully build a culture where the remaining people value forced ranking. In my experience, you create a cutthroat culture based on resource efficiency, not a culture of collaboration based on flow efficiency.

When you rank people, the culture reinforces the idea that *who* gets ahead matters more than excellent outcomes for the customers.

If you continue to force rank, you create a culture where:

- People work to protect themselves, not to create great products.
- People work to maximize their review/evaluation, not for the good of the company or the product.
- People stop taking risks because it's not safe to experiment and learn. If you make a mistake, you have a real risk of being fired.
- Managers consciously hire inadequate people so that they'll have someone to fire.

There's another side effect of ranking people. Some managers think they can fire the bottom 5-10% of the "lowest" people.

Every manager I meet prides him or herself on hiring the best people. If you hired the best people, why would you fire any of them?

I suspect that most organizations that use "rank-and-yank" use this practice to manage salaries. Rank and yank does not create employee engagement. Rank and yank reinforces cynical people—people who are out for themselves and no one else.

I'll discuss ways to manage salary expenses later in this chapter.

Too many performance management activities create employee *disengagement.* It's not difficult to create engagement—start with meaning.

4.4 What Creates Employee Engagement?

I've asked plenty of people why they work. They all agree they need a fair wage. Some people like to be a part of something greater than themselves. Several people told me it was the company's mission, the purpose. (See Start With Why on page 4.)

Some people told me they wanted to be a part of a high-performing team. Again, something greater than themselves. Some people told me they wanted a chance to learn something "important" that they could use to extend their skills in some way.

Engaged people work for autonomy, mastery, and purpose, as Dan Pink said in *Drive: The Surprising Truth About What Motivates Us* [PIN11].

If you believe the people you serve are adults, you don't need to manage anyone's performance. You might need to consider your actions for how to create an environment in which people can succeed:

- You might have to define or refine the organization's strategy or mission so people know why you asked them to work on *this* product or project or experiment.
- You might have to manage the project portfolio so people focus on one and only one project or product.
- You might have to offer feedback and coaching or assist others in offering that feedback and coaching.

I recommend you find a way to offer reinforcing feedback as often as possible.

It seems so easy. Offer people a purpose greater than themselves. Offer people autonomy in their team or their work. Offer people a chance to learn, to increase their mastery. When you offer purpose, autonomy, and mastery, people become and stay engaged.

This is easy for me to say. You might have to work against your current culture or environment to do this.

People disengage when they don't have autonomy, mastery, and purpose.

We still need to manage salary expenses and offer people meaningful work.

4.5 Options to Manage Salary Expenses

We have several ways to manage salary expenses:

- A career ladder, so people understand their levels.
- A salary structure for a specific job level.
- A separate, profit-sharing bonus, especially if the organization has more profit at the end of the fiscal year.

And, if you can create a safe-enough environment, consider asking people how they feel about making all salary information public.

Too often, career ladders are about technical and functional skills, not interpersonal skills. The more innovation you want in an organization, the more interpersonal skills count.

4.5.1 *Create Career Ladders*

People—the people you lead and serve—provide outcomes. The outcomes they provide this year are more difficult than the outcomes you needed one, two, or five and more years ago.

Because the outcomes differ, your job as a manager is to facilitate the team's learning so they can achieve new and more challenging outcomes. I like to ask this question: How can you help those people learn together, to become a product of their joint learning? (See *Symmathesy: A Word in Progress* [BAT15].)

The more people learn together, the more they learn to master the interpersonal skills they need for their current team. And, the more teams they experience, the more they learn to apply those skills with more people.

That means managers rarely want to encourage a linear career. (If someone wants a linear career, that's fine. You don't have to encourage it.) The more you can encourage a jungle gym approach to a career, the more likely people are to enjoy their work. (See *Lean In: Women, Work, and the Will to Lead* [SAN13] for the first place I saw the idea of a jungle gym for a career.)

As an employee, I used the career ladders to see where I wanted to expand my circle of influence. As a manager, you can influence the career ladder at your organization to focus on the interpersonal skills you want to encourage: collaboration with others, facilitating the difficult choices in the product and the team, adaptability, resilience, and other non-technical skills.

Career ladders, especially as a jungle gym, help people realize they don't need to become a manager to get the next promotion.

Does your organization have a career ladder for all the jobs, including exempt (salaried), non-exempt (hourly), and all management?

If not, how can people see where they might want to expand their skills?

I designed my career—and my managers appreciated my initiative. Can you help other people design their career, given the constraints of the work you need them to accomplish? The people might need training and coaching to achieve those new results.

Technical skills are relatively easy to learn and master. (See *Hiring Geeks That Fit* [ROT12] for more details.)

The interpersonal skills matter more for innovation than technical expertise. Formal education or certifications are practically irrelevant in an organization focused on innovation. That's because the team learns together, and the managers learn together in flow efficiency.

I have found that continuing education works for many people, including me. I expand my knowledge and experiment with new ideas. If the people you serve want to use that education to obtain a degree or a certificate, terrific. Don't assume a degree or a certificate actually creates that learning.

If your organization does not yet have a career ladder, use interpersonal skills as the basis for a career ladder. (See "Creating Agile HR", Part 5: Performance Management, the Career Ladder[1] for an example of a career ladder.)

Once you have a career ladder, you can create a reasonable salary structure for each level.

4.5.2 *Create a Salary Structure for Each Level*

A salary structure based on a career ladder can help the organization manage salary parity. And, the salary structure allows people to see and understand how much value they offer the organization.

We all have access to how other organizations organize their salary structures and pay for each part of the career ladder. Glassdoor.com and

---

[1] https://www.jrothman.com/mpd/agile/2017/08/creating-agile-hr-part-5-performance-management-the-career-ladder/

other salary sites make some of that information transparent. And, HR can subscribe to various reports that offer various data.

A salary structure is not a panacea. However, the more knowledge people have about the salaries, and the more they see the career levels, the more influence they have on their career and their pay.

If we have reasonable levels and a fair salary, why do so many organizations offer individual bonuses for team-based work?

4.6 Individual Bonuses Create Disengagement

I've seen way too many organizations manage their salary expenses by creating a payment package. The employee receives a smaller amount of base pay, and then—a year later—the employee earns a substantial bonus, assuming the person or the company meets objectives.

In reality, that's deferring a substantial portion of what should be a person's reasonable salary, so the organization has the use of that money for longer. That's incongruent with Create Integrity in the Organization on page 20.

Individual bonuses don't make sense. If we're going to encourage flow efficiency throughout the organization, we need to rethink bonuses. Here are the specific issues with using bonuses as a way to create engagement:

- In team-based work, we can't untangle any single person's performance from that of the rest of the team. We can't disentangle a manager's contribution either, because the managers collaborate across the organization and support the team's environment.
- Waiting a year to offer a bonus is a too-long cadence for employee engagement.
- Too many bonuses are out of the control of the person who's supposed to receive the bonus.

Let's first start with the idea that we can somehow understand what a given person does and untangle those actions from the rest of the team.

4.6.1 *We Can't Understand Each Person's Contribution*

If your organization wants to use flow efficiency for innovation, you can't tell who has done which work—alone. We each have good days and bad days.

When we work in flow efficiency, our team helps us succeed. When someone has a bad day, we support that person. When someone has a great day, that person might accelerate the entire team. It's not possible to count every person's good days and bad days.

And, since Environment Shapes Everyone's Behavior (page 10), we are much less likely to be able to create our good days and bad days.

Is there a reasonable way to compensate people for individual work?

The team always knows who has done what. They might not realize how people contribute. For example, the team might not know how much they needed Amy's facilitation or Paul's willingness to experiment. The team always knows when someone isn't contributing enough.

The manager can try to learn by asking for status or accomplishments. But the team knows.

The more a team collaborates, the less we know about any given person's contribution.

4.6.2 *Too Long a Cadence*

If we want a bonus to help employee engagement, why wait until the end of a year? Why not keep the reward closer to the actual achievement?

If your organization believes in a yearly cadence, they are managing their salary expenses, not offering recognition or a reward for great work.

4.6.3 *Is Your Bonus Under Your Control?*

I rarely see a bonus under the control of the person who's supposed to receive that bonus.

You may have a bonus based on management by objectives: "We'll increase our sales by x% over this year." All department and personal objectives flow from that statement. Too often, those objectives focus on a manager's function (not a cross-functional team). Once the objective reaches a person, the bonus is contingent on specific *outputs*.

Very few people can control their actions or their outputs to achieve those bonuses.

I also don't recommend OKRs for bonuses. I'll talk about OKRs as a way to guide what to choose to do and not do in Verify the Team's Objectives (page 61).

Bonuses do not offer employee engagement. See *Drive: The Surprising Truth About What Motivates Us* [PIN11], *Dangerous Half-Truths, and Total Nonsense: Profiting from Evidence-based Management* [PFS06], and *Beyond Budgeting: How Managers Can Break Free from the Annual Performance Trap* [HOF03].

Even If you manage salespeople, consider the sales team. I often see sales teams with a lead salesperson, sales engineers, and possibly an in-house salesperson. That's a team approach to sales. If you lead independent salespeople, you might have to offer a reasonable salary with a small bonus for *delivering* sales. If you only compensate salespeople on closing sales, they might sell future deliveries, not what your products can deliver *now*.

Instead of individual bonuses, decide how you might share profits. See how evenly you can distribute those profits. There are many traps for profit-sharing:

- Assuming some people, such as senior managers, deserve a substantial part of the profit.
- Too-small salaries, assuming people will receive the profit sharing as a "bonus."
- How to handle compensation when people take a sabbatical or a leave.
- The way many organizations pay senior managers.

You might not be the person to decide how the compensation system will work. However, when you realize how it creates dysfunction and disengagement, you can start the discussions.

4.7 Options to Create Engagement

What can you do to create engagement?

Start with the principles in Consider These Innovation Leadership Principles (page 1) and apply them in these ways:

1. As a manager, create overarching and specific goals for each team or function, depending on your organization. Make sure you clarify the "why" behind those goals.
2. Offer the team/people sufficient autonomy to deliver the work. Clarify any specific guidelines or constraints, such as an upper bound for cost.
3. Ask people to learn with each other and show you their progress.

If you do that, people work for autonomy, mastery, and purpose. They generate their engagement.

Consider bonuses when the organization can share profits and when people have shown more initiative that helps everyone perform better. You can ask the team or wait for the team to tell you. The more you work in flow efficiency, the more the team knows how everyone works.

You don't have to manage anyone's performance, especially not for engagement. The people you serve are not puppets on a stage. They are thinking, capable people who will deliver if you help create an environment where they can engage.

CHAPTER 5

Which Teams Are the Best?

Years ago, I assessed an IT organization of about 1500 people. The leaders thought everyone in IT knew how to do everything in IT. IT included security teams, application teams, and office build-out teams.

The security teams worked both proactively and reactively. They planned their proactive work for the various security measures and monitoring software for their network and devices. They couldn't plan their reactive work. They reacted to threats and added more monitoring as they learned about the threats.

The application teams created some internal applications and customized and supported other applications. They also responded to production support issues across all the applications. They were able to plan most of their work, except for the production support work.

The office build-out teams were able to plan most of their work in advance. Except when the local internet suppliers didn't respond in time. Or, when a builder didn't start on time. Or, when the local inspectors weren't available to give an occupancy certificate in time.

All three kinds of teams were able to plan a little and respond a little. And, all three kinds of teams had different needs for their planning and response times.

The managers wanted to measure each team against a standard: the team's variance to the schedule. Why? Managers wanted to "scale" the organization—to determine where to add more people and teams.

I asked the leaders if the schedules were comparable. Did outfitting new office space compare to keeping invaders off the network? How important was each schedule?

No, the schedules weren't comparable. And, most of the time, the schedules weren't even that important. Especially not for the security people. They had to respond to various network attacks, not keep to a schedule. Even the schedules for the application teams and office build-out work had some flexibility.

I asked the leaders what value they thought they would gain by comparing the teams. The leaders thought they needed to manage performance. (See Must We Manage Performance? on page 39.) Instead, the managers needed to learn about flow efficiency and how to clarify the organization's purpose.

I learned something quite important about each team. Each team wanted to know how they could contribute to the betterment of the whole organization.

The teams already worked as best as they could. And, the teams monitored their work. The teams knew what they needed to do: to improve.

The managers didn't need to—and could not—compare teams. The teams didn't do the same kind of work.

What about teams that *look* like they perform the same work? For example, I see many programs (a collection of projects with one business deliverable that requires all the teams) where teams work on their own feature sets. Can we compare those teams?

My experience is that comparing teams doesn't add value to the *product*. This is the same problem as comparing people in the organization. That's because most of a team's (or a person's) performance is a function of the environment. See Environment Shapes Everyone's Behavior (page 10).

Comparing teams is not valuable for anyone—especially not managers.

5.1 Myth: I Can Compare Teams and It's Valuable to Do So

Barry, a senior director in a large organization, puzzled over the problem. He wasn't sure how to see his department's progress as a whole. He was sure some teams were much less effective than other teams. He texted Sam, a colleague and asked for a meeting.

Later that day, Barry strode into Sam's office. "Hey Sam, I need to see how my teams are doing—compared to each other. How do you compare teams?"

"I don't compare teams," said Sam. "Why are you trying to compare teams?"

"So I can tell who's being more productive and who's slacking off," Barry replied. "But I thought for sure you did this. You always seem to have really productive teams. How do you measure them?"

"I don't measure them," Sam said.

"What do you mean you don't measure them? You must do something. How else will you know if the teams are any good? How about the people on the teams? You must measure them. Come on, what's your secret?" Barry asked.

"I don't measure a thing about the people. I don't measure the teams' output. I set product goals with them. We decide on a higher-level objective and jointly decide on product or other measures. And, I ask the teams to measure their *throughput* and to ask me for help if they are unhappy with their throughput," Sam said.

Barry looked up at the ceiling. "Hmm. Higher-level goals, that's your secret? Do you use OKRs, Objectives and Key Results?"

Sam said, "I don't use OKRs anymore. I had trouble because people tried to cascade them down to teams and individuals." He shrugged. "That wasn't what I wanted. So I keep an organizational goal, and that seems to work."

Barry nodded.

Sam said, "My job is to help create the environment that will allow our team members to work in a reasonable way. I make sure they know which project is number one. I arrange for training for people when my managers tell me people need training. I make sure everyone knows our mission, why we exist. And, I make sure they know this quarter's objective. But I don't bother with that comparison nonsense. Is someone asking you to compare teams?"

Barry shook his head. "Well, no, but I have no idea how to know who is doing great work and who's not doing so well. I have engineering teams here in California and some in Colorado. I have some teams in France and some in Israel and Bangalore. How do I compare them? They are cross-functional teams. They work on the same product. You would think I would be able to compare them. But I can't figure out how."

"Okay, let's deconstruct this," Sam said. "First, why do you want to? What's the value you obtain from comparing teams? What would change if you suddenly know one team is better—which I'm not saying you will discover. But if you did discover that, what would you do?"

Barry thought for a few minutes. "Well," he said, "I'd reward that team."

Sam shook his head. "No, you wouldn't. Not if you wanted that team to work with the other teams on the program ever again. The teams have to collaborate. Why would you pit the teams against each other?"

"Because I want to get the best out of my people," replied Barry.

"Okay, that's a great goal," said Sam. "I also want to get the best out of my people. I tell them what the best is. The best is often a specific release date for the product. It might be some release criterion since we're in engineering. When I ran support, it was something else. When I ran IT, it was performance for the organization. But it was never a measurement for the team. Never. I only use measures based on what I call a "superior" goal, the organization's overarching goal."

Barry sat back and sighed. "I didn't realize."

"If you want to measure something, you might start with yourself. You're at the top of your department. But that doesn't make sense either, does it?"

Barry shook his head.

Sam said, "You can't directly measure the performance of a team. However, you can measure the team's accomplishments and maybe their learning. At one point, I measured features-per-unit-time, and I discovered people gamed that measure. They made the features smaller. I'd temporarily forgotten Goodhart's Law, "When a measure becomes a target, it ceases to be a good measure." He chuckled.

"Was that a problem?" Barry asked.

"No, that was actually a great thing. But I don't just want features. I want finished products. That's why measuring features instead of progress towards organizational goals doesn't make sense. At least, not to me. I tell people what I want. For engineering, I explain about the impact on customers. For support, it's about retention and customer satisfaction. I tell them what I want.

Barry said, "I don't know. I just don't know."

"Look," Sam said. "Do you think people come to work to do a bad job?"

"No," Barry said.

"So, treat them as if they come to work to do a great job," Sam said. "They will live up to your expectations. But you have to do your part. You have to tell them what you want. That's why I find the idea of overarching goals useful right now."

Barry nodded.

Sam continued, "I also provide any necessary resources, provide training, and have one-on-ones with my managers. I work through my managers to provide meta-coaching and feedback. The managers remove the impediments—or I do, depending on the problem."

Barry said, "Makes sense. I'm already doing that."

"Yup," Sam said. "Now, all you need to do is add in the high-level objectives, through OKRs. Or, some other overarching goal. We don't need to measure people or teams or compare them."

Barry nodded. "It sounds simple when you say it like that."

Sam smiled. "It's not simple to do," he said. "But you don't have to measure the teams. There's no value in that. If you think there is, measure yourself first. See what you discover. Then apply your measurement to your teams."

5.2 Individuals and Teams Perform Incomparable Work

Managers want to know which teams are the most effective. Managers think they can learn from the teams doing better and support other teams to apply those learnings.

That sounds reasonable, doesn't it?

We have several problems with this seemingly reasonable goal. The first problem is that because teams perform incomparable work, we don't have a single set of measures that would help us see a team's success from data.

However, an even larger problem is that a person's—and by extension, a team's—behavior is a function of their environment. (See Environment Shapes Everyone's Behavior on page 10.)

We can use qualitative measures to assess the culture via Hofstede's cultural dimensions. (See *Cultures and Organizations: Software of the Mind 3rd ed* [HHM10].) We can assess psychological safety. (See *Teaming: How Organizations Learn, Innovate, and Compete in the Knowledge Economy* [EDM12].)

Qualitative data offers us valuable insights into how teams work—especially if we use that information to remove obstacles for the teams. For example, Project Aristotle tells us there is a correlation between psychological safety and a team's performance[1]. (Project Aristotle also collected a variety of qualitative and quantitative measures for each team.)

---

[1] https://rework.withgoogle.com/guides/understanding-team-effectiveness/steps/introduction/

However, we don't have quantitative data that allows us to *easily* assess teams. If you want to repeat the Project Aristotle data gathering for yourself, you'll need to spend time creating *your* measures of effectiveness.

And, sometimes, managers want to measure teams to reward the "best" teams and eliminate or impose changes on the "worst" teams.

Even when teams work on the same product, they work in different areas of the product. Every team has different work.

In software product development, we know a little about what makes it impossible to compare the work of any two teams:

- The requirements differ for different areas of the product. The requirements are not comparable between teams. When teams work on different products altogether, the requirements are even less comparable.
- Each area has its own problem difficulty.
- Each area has its own initial state of code and tests. For example, a product area with more useful tests at all levels makes changing that area easier than an area with insufficient tests.

That's just software. What if we extend this wish to compare software product teams and marketing communication teams? I don't have any idea about how to compare those teams. They do different and necessary work for the organization's purpose, that overarching goal.

I can ask the team to measure their cycle time and look for delays and bottlenecks. That might help me, as a manager, support the different teams.

When we try to compare teams' performance, we treat each team as a resource. We use resource efficiency thinking for teams. Instead of resource efficiency, how can we use flow efficiency?

5.3 **Measure Flow, Not Productivity**

As long as I've worked, people have tried to measure the productivity of knowledge workers.

When I was a programmer, some of my managers measured lines of code. They didn't realize that I could easily game that measure by writing more lines—useful or not. Some of my more clever colleagues used to see how few lines of code they could write—whether anyone could read that code or not.

Some managers tried to measure testers by the number of tests they wrote or the defects they found. Those measures have the same problem as measuring lines of code.

I could continue, but I'll spare you. Measuring the number of problems fixed or meetings conducted—or almost anything where there's a single number—does not make sense for any measure of productivity. (Single dimension measurements invite people and teams to game the number and obfuscate reality. Multiple dimension measurements make the gaming more difficult but still possible.)

What does productivity mean to you? Can you define "best" for a team?

I prefer to measure something the customer can use or consume, an outcome. That might be a released, running, tested feature. Marketing might create a white paper about product performance. A customer can read that paper and make a decision.

However, let me caution you about interim outputs. For example, if a team creates a database schema but does not release any feature that uses that schema, I would not call that an outcome. Not yet.

Maybe you can start with yourself.

What kind of outcomes do you create as a manager? How do you affect what the customer sees and uses?

Because managers support and serve the people who make the product or service, and because the managers create and refine the environment, I do not know a way to measure managers.

I can measure the delays managers might create in the system. The more delays, the longer it takes for the makers to release outcomes.

And, consider how you depend on other managers to do their jobs. That's why when we Encourage Management Flow Efficiency (page 12), we look at the entire flow of work.

Just as we can't measure or compare teams, we can't directly measure managers, either.

You cannot measure what people *do* and expect that measure to be useful. Why? Because every innovative organization is a collaborative learning activity—a team sport. Everything we do depends on other people. (The more you need an innovative organization, the more you need to learn from each other.)

Knowledge workers—including managers—work together to create something more than any one person could provide. All the work they do is interconnected. That means that when we measure flow, we create a better measure than some piece of the whole.

Instead of comparison, specify the outcomes or objectives you want.

5.4 Verify the Team's Objectives

Do all the teams you serve know their objectives? I know of two ways to create those objectives: OKRs and corporate objectives.

Some people find OKRs a useful framework to define the objective with measurable results. You define a big picture and—often, audacious—objective. Then the teams create their Key Results.

Don't expect any team or teams to accomplish all the results. Supposedly, if the teams can achieve the results, you didn't define an audacious enough objective. For more depth, see *Radical Focus: Achieving Your Most Important Goals with Objectives and Key Results* [WOD16] and *Measure What Matters: How Google, Bono, and the Gates Foundation Rock the World with OKRs* [DOE18].

If you decide to use OKRs, consider them as something significant for the whole business. The more significant the objective, the more you answer the "why" question. I link the objective to the overall why, as in Start With Why (page 4).

Consider These Guidelines for OKRs

I've seen OKRs trip up too many managers and management teams. To avoid those problems, read the books I recommend and consider these guidelines:

Set one bold, inspirational objective for the company. If you're organized into divisions, set an objective for the division. If you can't create one objective that covers a division, don't start with OKRs. Clarify your division's purpose first.

Now that you have one objective, create three Key Results. For example, if you think you might want to change the revenue model, you might create an objective of "Establish New Product X as the premier product in its category."

You would then create Key Results that span the organization. For example, you might have a Key Result about creating and publishing benchmarks. Product development and marketing might share that key result. You might have another Key Result about showing the product at a tradeshow. To achieve that result, product development, sales, and marketing might have to collaborate to achieve the result.

If you create OKRs that start with a focus on one part of the organization, you don't have OKRs. You have MBOs (Management by Objectives). Instead of starting with OKRs, start with the principles in Consider These Innovation Leadership Principles (page 1).

OKRs can work. Yet, most of my clients use them the way they use MBOs, Management By Objectives. They start with a big Objective. Then, they cascade the objectives or key results down to the teams— and often to individual people. That's not how OKRs are supposed to work.

When Drucker wrote about MBOs, the objective was a company-wide objective, not a personal objective. He called this "Management by objectives and self-control." These are quotes from Drucker, *The Essential Drucker* [DRU01]:

- "Business performance . . . requires that each job be directed toward the objectives of the whole business."
- ". . . each manager's job must be focused on the success of the whole."

Drucker's MBOs were not the personal goals that my managers attempted to use. Drucker originated OKRs.

I'm not sure you need OKRs or other formal objectives, as long as the organization clarifies its purpose. And, as long as every project or product somehow focuses on that purpose.

Instead of comparing teams, consider supporting teams to be their best.

5.5 Options To Support Teams to be Their Best

Instead of trying to compare teams, let's go up a level. Why do you want to measure teams?

I've seen these useful reasons:

- Discover when teams are in trouble so you can support them.
- See if teams are stuck.
- See if the team has a healthy ability to discuss their work and their challenges.

You might have another reason, focused on supporting the people you lead.

In my experience, people and teams don't need *direct* measurement to be their best. Consider these ideas to help teams be their best:

1. Clarify the team's purpose.

2. Ask teams and managers to work in flow efficiency. When the entire organization works to a single purpose, the organization succeeds.

3. Make sure you have decriminalized mistakes. If people have a chance to make mistakes and recover from them, they will find ways to never make those mistakes again. They will experiment and innovate.

4. Decide if you want to invest the effort to measure your culture and the psychological safety of the teams. If so, you will gain much more benefit from that work than measuring teams directly.

CHAPTER 6

Does Competition Between Teams or Managers Work?

I meet too many managers who think a competitive environment *inside* the organization leads to more creativity.

That competition takes several forms. I've seen product managers have to compete for the available teams—instead of the organization creating a project portfolio. One reason this occurs is that the organization has not rationalized its *product* portfolio—the list of products and services the organization wants to offer and support. Another reason might be that the organization focuses on too-small chunks of work instead of optimizing for a superior product goal. The result is that the organization has an appetite for more products than it has teams to finish that work. The organization cannot rationalize its *project* portfolio.

I've seen the same problem in IT organizations where Finance makes the case they should get a team instead of HR. It's the portfolio problem again. And, when HR or a senior manager asks managers to rank everyone—that's another form of competition.

When you create competition inside an organization, you create zero-sum games.

Zero-sum games have only one winner. Everyone else loses. Often, the person who wins is the person who creates the ranking or competition. And, zero-sum games create friction in the organization because people don't optimize for the overarching goal:

- Everyone works in resource efficiency. People tend to say, "That's not my job." Developers write more code because that's where they have expertise instead of testing or supporting testers. Managers focus on their silos instead of collaborating across the organization.

- People stop collaborating because they will lose the competition.
- That lack of collaboration causes people to lose all psychological safety. People stop trusting and respecting each other.

When managers create competition, they lose their management integrity over time. Management loses all integrity over time.

Competition inside the organization is a bad idea. And, because too many managers still believe in competition, too many organizations create competitive situations. The result? The organization loses product coherence and collaboration, and everything takes longer to achieve.

6.1 Myth: Friendly Competition Is Constructive

"Jonah and Sarah, this next round, I want to initiate a little competition to see whose team can develop the best product. Won't that be fun?" Dave, the VP of engineering, rubbed his hands with glee. "OK, what's next on the agenda?"

Sarah looked at Jonah. "Dave, we're not done with this agenda item yet. If you want the best product, why don't we collaborate instead of compete?"

"Well, everyone knows that friendly competition makes the best products, right?"

"Well, *I* don't know that," Sarah said. "When I look at our outcomes when we work in flow efficiency, I see faster and better results."

"I don't know that, either," Jonah said. "In fact, my team works really well with Sarah's team. I don't want to see us lose that ability to collaborate. What do you want to have happen here? A competition or the best product?"

Dave leaned back in his chair. "I want the best product, but I want it fast. I thought a little competition might speed things up."

Sarah leaned forward. "Then let us collaborate. We're really good together."

Jonah nodded. "Our teams like working together. Sometimes, it's like a super-team."

"Well, why don't we merge the teams and have just one team, then? Why do I need two managers, if your teams like working together so much?" Dave sounded confused.

"We need two teams because between the two of us, we serve more than thirty people. Jonah and I are already on the hairy edge of not serving the people we try to serve now," Sarah said.

Jonah nodded. "Right. We can manage them because, as agile teams, they are self-managing. We don't have one team underneath each of us—we have several teams 'underneath' us." He used air quotes.

Sarah nodded.

Jonah continued. "When our teams collaborate, they work on the backlog—sometimes the same backlog, sometimes different backlogs— all in service of the roadmap."

Dave leaned back and listened.

"Sarah and I have one-on-ones with our team members," Jonah said. "We help remove obstacles the project managers or team members can't remove themselves. We help the team members solve problems with intra-team communications. We don't solve problems for the team members that they can solve themselves. We facilitate the work of the people in the teams."

Sarah piped up. "If you made one team of thirty-three people, neither of us could 'manage' that many people. We couldn't have one-on-ones even biweekly. We couldn't remove obstacles or solve problems, whatever you would like to call it. It's just too many."

Dave nodded. "Ah, okay," he said.

"Currently, we each have several teams of four to seven people doing the technical work," she said. "Many of those teams collaborate with each other to make products for the good of the company, and we encourage that."

Jonah continued. "If you want these collaborative teams to compete, we can't stop you. But, it's a terrible idea. Instead, tell the teams what you want—a great product—then let *them* decide how to do it. You might even say, 'I thought about having a competition. Do you think that's a good idea?', then see what they think of that idea. But don't mandate it."

Sarah said, "You hired these people because they can think and produce. Let them."

"Let's compete with our competitors and collaborate inside the organization," Jonah said.

Sarah nodded. "Now, did we convince you internal competition is not such a good idea?" Sarah wanted to make sure Dave understood.

"Yes, you did. I got it. Okay, *now* can we go onto the next agenda item?" Dave shook his head. "What would I do without you all?"

Sarah laughed. "You'd make mistakes. That's why you have us."

Dave, Jonah, and Sarah all laughed.

6.2 "Friendly" Competition Never Is

When managers decide to introduce competition between teams, it's rarely a "friendly" competition to create a great product. There are winners and losers. Those on the losing team often have a surprise waiting for them on their performance evaluations.

Most knowledge work is about learning. In product development, we learn by experimenting. That means we need to expect failures. If we think of failure as learning, the key is to learn as fast as possible, not slowly.

When teams or people decide on their own to have a friendly competition, they learn together. That's because it's peer-based. Instead of a reward or a performance evaluation, peers improve their mastery of their craft, egging each other on. Everyone wins.

6.3 What Are Your Objectives?

If you think you want a "friendly" competition between or among teams, consider first defining your objectives. Do you want a great product? If so, make sure each team works on just this product. When you do, everyone focuses on that product.

Then, consider asking the teams if they want to collaborate. You might ask the teams to brainstorm ways in which they collaborate. They will have many ideas—more than just competition.

Don't try to compare the teams based on their *activities*. Instead, create an outcomes-based rubric by which everyone can evaluate the solutions for their approach to a great product. Each team will develop solutions differently. Since you will see a different solution from each team, it's impossible to compare solutions—or teams.

Consider framing this product work as a series of experiments. Ask each team to experiment in as short a time period as possible. I like considering experiments that take a maximum of one week. Then, at the end of four weeks, we have results from many experiments. We can evaluate those results.

6.4 Ask the Teams for the Results You Want

Once you know your objectives, ask the teams for the results you want.

If you want a variety of solutions, tell the teams, and tell them why. Maybe you want to timebox possibilities. Perhaps you want to explore options for your clients or customers—or the future of your products. The more information you provide the teams about your objectives, the better the teams can fulfill your needs.

In any case, the more information the teams have, the better your outcomes will be.

You hired smart, capable people. Let them work in a way that proves how smart they can be.

If you are worried about seeing deliverables, ask the teams to provide solutions or interim solutions inside a specific timebox. Teams, especially agile teams, are often willing to timebox solutions for you if you explain why.

TIP Management-based competition creates stress and anxiety, not better products.

Management-based competition does not help people perform better. Instead, tell people what you want and let them decide how to deliver. You will get the results you want, without the false structure of competition.

6.5 Recognize Competition

You might see management-based competition in these circumstances:

1. You have too few people or teams to finish all the necessary work. Your management team needs to collaborate on the project portfolio. (See Options to Collaborate on the Project Portfolio on page 116.)
2. Someone still thinks rank-and-yank is a good idea. (See Ranking People Creates Disengagement on page 44.)
3. Someone believes resource efficiency is a good idea, especially if these people believe the Myth: Performance Management Creates Employee Engagement on page 41).

Each of these circumstances has a different root cause.

If you have too few people or teams to finish all the work, your organization needs a different way to manage the project portfolio. (See *Manage Your Project Portfolio: Increase Your Capacity and Finish More Projects, 2nd ed* [ROT16] for details.)

If managers still want to manage via resource efficiency, discover why.

If your managers want competition, ask the managers to ask the teams to create competitions the teams will enjoy.

6.6 Options to Avoid Competition

If you think I'm nuts and that competition is a great idea, consider this self-reflection:

1. Think back to the most recent work-based competition in which you participated. During the competition, how did people treat

each other? What did people discuss during the competition, inside their teams, and across teams?

2. After the competition, how did people treat each other? What did they discuss inside their teams and across teams?

3. What was the product or service outcome? How easy was it to select which product won? What effect did that product have on the market?

4. Did that product have the results you expected? How expensive is it to support that product?

5. Especially if you've had time to reflect on that experience, can you imagine three other ways to achieve the results you wanted?

When people and teams work for an overarching goal in flow efficiency, they tend to create better products in a shorter time. I have yet to see competition work.

Consider these ideas to avoid competition:

1. Make sure your managers collaborate to create one project portfolio across the organization.

2. Create short experiments instead of projects. Remember to judge an experiment by how quickly people and teams learn, not whether they achieved "success." The learning determines success. That will help managers evaluate outcomes so they can plan the next steps.

3. Use the Rule of Three to generate at least two other options aside from creating competition. (See Increase Management Capability on page 27 for more details.)

4. Ask the teams to create competitions they might enjoy—a competition for a superior outcome.

CHAPTER 7

What Kind of
Physical Space Works?

Several years ago, an Engineering VP explained he was worried about his retention rate. The company had recently moved to a new space. Before this move, the department had retained more than 90% of the people. Now, a year after the move, the retention rate had dropped to 65%. That was a significant increase in the number of people leaving.

I asked what had changed. New managers? No. New products? No. I asked for a tour of the space.

I saw rows and rows of tables in a large loft. The space had originally been a warehouse, with very high ceilings, windows at least 15 feet high, and exposed brick and ceilings.

The original tenant had installed fluorescent lights that flickered every so often and hummed the entire time I was there. The air ventilation system fans were quite noisy.

While the brick walls looked great, they amplified the general noise in the room.

The place certainly had "atmosphere." However, the entire space suffered from insufficient light and too much noise.

People had modern-looking chairs, but not ergonomic chairs. I saw several shorter women who propped their feet up on stools under the table so they could position their chairs high enough to reach their keyboards.

I started to count the number of people with hand and wrist supports or braces. I counted to ten and stopped.

People sat in functional groups, not cross-functional teams. The only whiteboards were in the conference rooms, and because the managers also sat at these long tables, the managers spent almost all of their time in the conference rooms for their necessary private conversations.

It's almost as if they designed the space to avoid collaboration.

I explained what I saw. I asked if the people who'd left had complained about physical discomfort. Yes, they had.

I have never seen a large contiguous space succeed, but maybe you have. I do know that knowledge workers require several kinds of space to effectively work alone and together. We need some concentration space. We need some collaboration space.

7.1 Myth: We Only Need One Kind of Space

Deb, a Director in an Engineering organization, stood outside her VP's cubicle, ready for her one-on-one. After being in this new space for a month, she had plenty to discuss with her VP, Carl.

Carl motioned her in. He had his headset on and was speaking with this hand over his mouth. He put his phone on mute and said to her, "I'll be available in a minute."

She shook her head and put a sticky on his desk. The sticky said, "Meet me in Conference Room 1. I have it booked for an hour."

Deb turned and walked away.

Carl frowned and ended his call. He arrived in Conference Room 1 a few minutes later. "A conference room for a one-on-one?" he asked. "Is this a big deal?"

"It is," Deb said. "Did you happen to notice the people in the cubes out there?"

"I did," Carl said. "Everyone's working, heads down, focused on their work."

"Yeah," Deb said. "Do you have any idea how many people are interviewing with other companies?"

Carl leaned back and said, "No. I had no idea that was a problem."

"It's a big problem," Deb said. "More than half of my department is interviewing. I didn't intentionally look, but almost all of them have changed their social media status to 'open for new opportunities.' You know what that means."

"Yup," Carl said. "We'll lose them soon unless we do something. Do you have any idea why they're looking for new jobs?"

"The damn cubicles," Deb said. "We no longer have any common space, such as a cafeteria. No one has an office. And, the conference rooms are so booked—I had to book this one a week ago. No one has space to collaborate. No one meets each other. You and the VPs were so focused on reducing our footprint that no one talks to each other at all."

"What's wrong with cubicles?" Carl said.

"Where do you collaborate with the other VPs?" Deb asked.

"In a conference room," he said.

"Yup, I collaborate with the other directors in a conference room, too," Deb said. "Where do you think the teams collaborate?"

"Let me guess," Carl said. "We take all the conference rooms so they have no place to go."

"Yup," Deb said. "Most of my team works from home as often as they can. Which isn't a problem, except we're not set up for people to work from home *and* build collaboration across the organization. IT doesn't like people working from home. Every time I request a few collaboration tools, they tell me they can't do that."

"I can fix that part," Carl said. "I understand where IT is coming from, but we need people to be able to work from home."

"That's only part of the point," Deb said. "We need serendipity so people can make connections and discover more about the products. When you took away the offices, people had no way to work in small groups or teams. And, when you took away the cafeteria, no one had a place to casually meet other people. And, now with this open floor plan, if anyone wants to discuss anything, everyone hears it."

"Is that all?" Carl asked, a slight smile on his face.

"Look," Deb said. "I realize you did this because we spent 'too much' on rent, but we used to have a gazillion new ideas a week. Now, we don't have any new ideas at all. People aren't discovering interesting things about the rest of the product. We're not collaborating. We have the worst of all possible worlds."

Carl shook his head. "Guess we screwed up."

"We can fix this," Deb said. "But, we need a wide variety of space. Teams need space to work together. We need room to learn in communities. And, we need informal space, where people might just strike up a conversation. And, we need serendipity."

"Serendipity?" Carl asked.

"Yeah," Deb said. "When was the last time you had a light bulb moment? An idea that came out of nowhere?"

Carl rubbed his chin. "I don't remember."

"Yeah," Deb said. "Me neither. I'm pretty sure we haven't had any of those great ideas because we're not set up to have them. We're reinforcing what we know and who we know. Not learning and meeting across the organization. We're going to get pretty stupid, soon."

Carl grinned. "Well, let's see if we can prevent stupid."

7.2 Knowledge Workers Need a Variety of WorkSpaces

I've found that people need a variety of spaces to do their best work: one-on-one space, team workspace, concentration space, serendipity space, and larger spaces for learning, where they can meet as a community or for workshops. That's a lot of pressure to put on the building architects, who usually don't understand what various knowledge workers do.

(TIP) People need a variety of workspaces to succeed.

You can manage some of these needs with effective remote work. Some virtual workspaces can take the place of in-person spaces. (See *From Chaos to Successful Distributed Agile Teams: Collaborate to Deliver* [ROK19].)

For example, in my work with remote teams, when the organization purposefully creates a virtual workspace where everyone has access to all the tools, the team can collaborate better than when each person is in an office wearing headphones.

One team moved from one-hour timeboxed meetings at work to virtual 25-minute meetings. They changed their meetings because they had more collaboration time virtually than they did in the office. And, they moved to shorter discussions because they could create smaller experiments. The conference room time does not limit how they can discuss their work.

This team used their virtual backchannel to check in with each other while they experimented. They found they could work faster when they weren't at the office—all because they didn't need to wait for a conference room.

Another team discovered they could have virtual coffee by choice. They invited other teams to their "Coffee Channel" in their collaboration tool. Soon, the Coffee Channel spawned other channels, where people could discuss everything from test architecture and automation to waterskiing. The informal channels helped people see each other as humans, which reinforced discussions across the organization about the work.

All the successful remote teams I've encountered meet with each other several times a year. They need both remote and in-person workspaces. They need virtual and in-person learning spaces.

7.3 How Knowledge Workers Use Space

If you've been in management a while, you might not realize how people now work. Let's take the case of Dan the Developer on a team that collaborates but does not work together all the time:

9 A.M.: Dan arrives at work. He checks his various communication channels. Solo, concentration work. He has a cubicle with low walls. He uses a headset because the cubicle walls actually seem to amplify his words across the entire room.

10 A.M.: Dan chooses the specific work for today. He works heads-down, reading the code, reading the tests, adding a test here and there. He might research online. More solo concentration work at his desk with his headset on.

11 A.M.: Dan has several questions for other developers and testers. He uses the team virtual backchannel to ask the questions so the other people can choose when to answer him. He's at his desk and uses a team virtual backchannel to communicate with his team.

11:45 A.M.: Dan has a standup just before lunch. The team meets in a small conference room. They don't have specific team space, but they've learned to work it out. Dan misses the immediacy of creating their progress charts on the wall, but he's learned to live with it.

Noon: Dan has lunch in the company cafeteria. He encounters people from another team and one of them helps him see an alternative solution to his problem. (This is an example of using the small-world network to everyone's benefit. See Figure 1.4: Small-World Network on page 15 to see an image of a small-world network.) The cafeteria creates serendipity for Dan to discover what other people do and know. (The organization also uses the cafeteria for learning events.)

1 P.M.: Back at his desk, Dan checks his backchannels to see who has replied to his questions. One of the other developers, Charlene, is available to pair. They use their virtual workspace to pair on his question first, then on hers. They're ready for a break a bit after 2:15. Each person sits at their own desk, and they collaborate in a virtual workspace. They each use a headset because they want to keep their voices low enough to avoid bothering other people.

2:15 P.M.: Dan and Charlene take a brief walk, continuing to talk about their various questions and work. Dan discovers another idea for their team's mobbing session this afternoon. Dan and Charlene work separately at their desks until 3 P.M.

3 P.M.: Dan and Charlene's team of seven people meets in a conference room for a mobbing session. Dan isn't excited about mobbing, but he admits he learns a ton this way. He still has to remind himself to speak up. The team has learned how to facilitate for all the introverts. He raises the topic he discovered with Charlene on their walk. Everyone can speak at a normal volume and not wear a headset.

5 P.M.: Dan finishes his work for the day. He's fixed a couple of small problems with the tests. He added a small feature and checked everything in. By 5:30 P.M, he's done and feels tired in a good way. He doesn't put his headset on again because he doesn't want to talk to anyone.

Dan worked alone at his desk. He also worked with Charlene virtually in a team workspace. He worked with his full team in the small conference room as an in-person collaborative space. He encountered someone he knew at lunch and got a great idea.

Also, note how many hours Dan used a headset both to keep noise from bothering him and to avoid bothering other people with his conversations.

If I had my way, everyone would have all of these spaces, both in-person and virtually:

- A private office for concentration work and to discuss items one-on-one or groups of three.
- A place to meet people without needing to make an appointment, such as a coffee area or a cafeteria.
- A team workspace that includes space to post data the team wants to track.
- A large workspace where teams can create or participate in workshops or communities of practice.

I know of very few organizations that offer all these spaces to every employee. Yet, when I speak with developers, testers, marketing people, product management people—everyone says they need a variety of workspaces.

7.4 Options to Create Necessary Workspaces

The wider the variety of workspaces, the more people can choose what's right for them and the work they do.

When we create workspaces that work for the specific work, we gain the benefits of focus, generating new ideas, and the ability to collaborate and finish work.

I've worked at home, in an office with a door, for 25 years. And, I still leave my office to interact with people. I gain ideas from those interactions.

I've learned to work virtually with people, writing books, and creating and delivering workshops. I also gain ideas from those interactions.

I have worked very hard to create virtual interactions that mimic in-person interactions. And, I still have to practice to create the back-and-forth that we find so easy in person. In person, we can often choose which space we want and then go there. In the virtual world, we have to decide in advance.

If you have a noisy office, create a virtual workspace so people can work somewhere they don't have to wear a headset to avoid the noise or collaborate. People need the option of working away from a noisy office. Sometimes, those people want to work from home. Sometimes, they want to escape the noise at the office. If you have not yet created the necessary infrastructure for people to work outside the office, do that now.

1. Ensure people have the necessary software tools to work from home at speed. That includes your VPN, remote access to all the applications, and sufficient meeting tools. People need both

a chat backchannel and video conferencing. (See *From Chaos to Successful Distributed Agile Teams: Collaborate to Deliver* [ROK19] for more details.)

2. Ask people what else they need for their in-office and remote workspace. Do people have enough monitors, sufficient ergonomic furniture, and anything else they need?

3. If you are still tied to a physical workspace, ask people what they need to think and work better. They likely know better than you. You might ask them to reflect on this question in a retrospective.

4. Ask people how often they want to work and learn together and to explain the space they need for those occasions.

CHAPTER 8

Don't We Need Estimates to Plan?

Several years ago, I drove into downtown Boston to work with a client on-site. I live about eight miles from the building. And, I was pretty sure it would take me between 30-60 minutes to drive there. I left the house on time and arrived in plenty of time to get a coffee.

The client's previous meeting ran late, so he met me a few minutes after our scheduled start. As we walked to his conference room, he asked me, "Why can't I get accurate estimates from our projects? I get estimates all over the map, and the reality is never the same as the prediction."

I asked him, "How long did you think the previous meeting would take, the one before this one?"

"An hour," he said.

"And, how long did it take?"

"About 75 minutes."

"If we have trouble planning meeting times when all we need to do is discuss a relatively known problem, how can we expect the projects to create great estimates?" I asked.

"But," he said, "the projects have known problems. They're dealing with . . ." his voice trailed off. "Ooh, I get it now. They're not dealing with known problems. In fact, the most interesting work is relatively unknown."

We can use estimates for the near term, and gross estimates—forecasts—for planning. (Daniel Vacanti in *When Will It Be Done?* [VAC18] uses the term "forecast.") Many people associate the term "forecast" with the weather. We know weather forecasts are pretty good for today and even for this week. Past that time, we expect updated forecasts as we learn more.

When we use the term forecast, we help people understand what they can get now: a reasonable prediction. While people might want a guaranteed estimate, a forecast is a better bet.

However, the more innovation you want, the fewer estimates you need. And, you might have training that says, "We need estimates to know how long the work will take!"

Here are some estimation facts from my years of experience:

- We make mistakes in the estimation units: If you estimate in days, you'll be off by days. If you estimate in weeks, months, quarters, or years, you are likely to be off by weeks, months, quarters, or years.
- Murphy's Law says we are likely to encounter problems more often than we can imagine. In my experience, things go wrong much more often than things go well.
- Many people assume they work a full eight-hour day. When I measure the effective hours of work at my clients, most people are lucky to get four hours of work in a day. Yet, people persist in planning for a "full" day.

We create bad estimates with our assumptions.

And, Daniel Kahneman in *Thinking Fast and Slow* [KAH11] explains the Planning Fallacy:

- We make plans and forecasts that are "unrealistically close to best-case scenarios."
- We can improve these plans by gathering statistics from similar situations.

Can tools help you? Maybe, if you use probabilities of actual data. For example, when you roll estimates up to create a project estimate, the completion date is the first date you can't *prove* the project won't be complete.

In this myth, I'm using the project portfolio as an example. If you plan quarterly for products based on the product roadmap, the same principles apply.

8.1 Myth: I Need Estimates to Plan

Susan, a CIO, had worked as a programmer, project manager, and then a manager. She'd become a CIO just last year. Her job now was to select the projects for the project portfolio for her part of the business.

She was frustrated. Over the past year, she'd asked teams for their project estimates so she could plan. The teams took weeks to calculate the estimate for just a quarter's worth of work. Then, when it came time to organize the project portfolio, she and her directors carefully slotted the projects into place. At the end of the quarter, every single team missed its estimate.

Then, she thought she'd look at all the time the teams spent estimating. Susan knew the teams spent an hour every two weeks planning the work for the next iteration. And, the teams refined the stories biweekly and estimated just a little, to understand the work they wanted to pull into the next iteration.

And, she suspected the teams—and the managers—spent about three weeks estimating for the next quarter. Susan knew all that time wasn't estimation, but she could use those times to create a ballpark estimate.

- Team time each week: about an hour each week for ten weeks in the quarter. That's ten hours per team, about a half week per team.
- Manager and team time each quarter preparing for the next quarter: about three weeks.

The total time: about three and a half weeks per team per quarter. That meant, in a given quarter, everyone spent almost one-quarter of their time in estimation activities. Not delivering or experimenting. Estimating. Across the entire organization.

No wonder that while the teams finished work, they couldn't finish everything they thought they could finish. It was time to meet with her directors.

The directors all filed in and sat down at the oval conference table.

"I want to know why our estimates are always wrong," Susan said. "I'm not blaming you for the incorrect estimates, but we need to understand what's wrong. I can't plan for a quarter."

Tim asked, "Why do we need to plan for a quarter? The teams are pretty good at planning for a couple of weeks. That's when the changes start. Why don't we plan for a month at a time?"

Susan thought for a few seconds. "Maybe," she said. "I'd really like to understand why first." On the far right side of the board, she wrote down "Plan for a month, max."

Andrea said, "My teams have a problem with new features being added to what we thought was stable for a quarter."

Susan asked, "So, we have scope creep—no, maybe it's actually scope realization—inside the quarter?"

"That might not be a real word," Andrea said and smiled. "And, yes. We realize what else we need to actually finish the work. The teams start with less-than-detailed requirements. So, as we have more conversations during the quarter, we discover more that we need to do to accomplish the outcomes we want."

Susan nodded.

Andrea continued, "We get so far into the work, and then we need a little more. And, because we've sort of played Tetris with all the projects, making sure the teams always have something to do, we don't have slack in the system."

"Ah," Susan said. "We're not asking people to multitask, but we're not leaving room for risks in our planning." She shook her head and then wrote "Scope realization" on the whiteboard. Then she asked, "What else?"

The directors listed several other root causes and compiled this list:

- "Scope realization," meaning the teams learned throughout the quarter.

- Insufficient risk management for what teams could do.
- Not enough slack in the system. No one team was overloaded, but all the teams had full backlogs.
- Some people got sick during the quarter, throwing off the estimates.
- Each team had a different level of accuracy in its estimates.
- Some teams didn't have good test automation at any level, so to maintain their technical excellence, they had to add tests.
- Some teams worked on something new to them every single quarter. They couldn't use their knowledge from the previous work or their previous estimations or cycle time.

As a team, Susan and her directors realized that estimating for a quarter was not going to work.

"Okay," Susan said. "I'll take ideas now. How do you want to fix this? I've got Tim's idea over here, plan for a month at a time. That would decrease our under-estimation errors."

The directors also suggested these ideas:

- Consider detailed estimates for a month and plan for a month at a time. The portfolio team would replan for the next month.
- Plan for a month, and then flow work into a team for the rest of the quarter. If a team finished work early, they could pull from the ranked project list. If a team looked like they would finish work later, ask the product person if the team needed to continue work on that backlog.
- Use spikes (short timeboxed experiments), design thinking, and other alternatives to make the work ready for the team so their estimate is more accurate. As a result, the team will rarely discover they need to do more work than they anticipated.
- Stop detailed estimating for planning purposes. Use a gross estimate—a forecast—for a quarter. That would take the pressure off the teams to develop accurate estimates. Susan and her team would think about how little they could do, instead of how much.

- Instead of estimates, talk about value and investing in the teams.

"Let's experiment with a month-long plan," Susan said, "and also talk about value. And, let's talk to the product people because that's a big issue. It doesn't make sense to ask about estimates when we don't know enough about the problems we want to solve."

8.2 Understand an Estimate's Value

Remember, an estimate is a guess. It is your best prediction of the future. And, if you estimate when the work is new to you, or at the start of a project, you know the least about the work when you're supposed to estimate it.

Even if you've done work similar to this work in the past, you might not know how dissimilar this work is from the past work. In Susan's organization, the teams often realized they needed more information about the work as they completed some of the work, what they called "scope realization." You might need a forecast or a ballpark estimate—in my experience, any more substantial estimate doesn't offer more value.

When we estimate, we try to predict the cost or time for some work. The more we know about our cycle time and the work, the more we can create reasonable estimates for short-term costs or time. Many teams find they can create realistic estimates for the next few days or a week, maybe two weeks. Once we try to create detailed estimates past that small amount of work, we often discover unknowns—which destroy our estimates.

We can also create forecasts or gross (not accurate) estimates for longer time periods, especially if we create and accept a range of dates. (See *Predicting the Unpredictable: Pragmatic Approaches to Estimating Project Schedule or Cost* [ROT15] for more guidance on ranges for forecasted dates.)

At the start of this chapter, I used a range of times for my travel time to Boston. I'd driven that route before, and the time varied from

30-60 minutes. I can assume it will take that time, but I can't be sure. (I might not encounter any traffic at all. Or, it might take me longer than 60 minutes if I encounter a very bad traffic accident that prevents me from getting off the highway to use surface streets.) The more data points I have, the more likely my estimate will be correct.

That day, I chose 45 minutes as my forecast, for a 75% confidence level. The more data I have about these drives, the better my forecast will be.

That's one event in an entire day. However, projects are a series of interrelated events. Projects are rarely just complicated. When something is complicated, we can still see the linear progression of the work. Projects are much more complex. Work is not linear and unknowns arise from "unrelated" events. We don't know what we don't know.

My client thought he could timebox his first meeting and meet me on time. However, as with many meetings of substance, the people in the meeting discovered more details they wanted to address at that time. In effect, they realized they needed to expand the scope—just a little.

They chose to ignore the timebox and do the work, there and then. (They had other choices, but they focused on management flow efficiency.)

All estimates have limited value because each estimate is so dependent on multiple factors, as in Susan's discussion with her directors. Susan and her directors described a complex adaptive system, with non-linear outputs and effects.

In order to create accurate estimates, we need to create these conditions:

- The team works together, limiting their WIP (Work in Progress).
- The team does not work on anything else, other than the work they choose. No one multitasks. No one does anything "extra" for anyone.
- The team has all the necessary tools and hard resources they require to complete the work.

If you can create those conditions, you don't need to estimate anything—assuming the team can deliver something every day or every other day. You have the perfect conditions for a team to deliver small-enough outcomes consistently.

Instead of estimates, you can use the work's value to make project portfolio decisions.

8.3 Plan by Value

Each project offers value in terms of deliverables or learning—or both. I often use these questions to help the portfolio team understand the value the project offers:

- How much do we want to invest in time, money, or learning before we stop?
- How can we see each team's progress so we can stop them when we don't want to invest more?
- What is the value of this project to us?

Aside from surfacing the sunk cost fallacy (using past investment to drive further investment), these questions help the portfolio team articulate the value, rather than the cost, of each project.

The portfolio team might say, "Please finish these three experiments for Project A—and please timebox your effort to three weeks." That means the portfolio team wants to invest three weeks of a project team for these experiments. The portfolio team knows the team's run rate, so they know how much three weeks will cost.

What if the project team can't complete the experiments in three weeks? That's an indication this work was more complex than the portfolio team anticipated—a form of data about the work. The portfolio team might want to see results before they add more time to the experiments.

And, if everyone specifically looks for outcomes, teams are more likely to create smaller pieces of work.

When we try to articulate the value of work, we might use the cost of delay, which helps us understand any urgency for the work, relative to the other work under consideration. (See *Manage Your Project Portfolio: Increase Your Capacity and Finish More Projects, 2nd ed* [ROT16] for ways to value the work.)

Value, not estimates, offers a portfolio team the ability to rank order the work without needing a prediction. And, when portfolio teams ask the investment question, they think about the work differently.

When you combine the investment question with more frequent evaluation of all the work in the project portfolio, the organization can pivot to different work more often. We have more planning flexibility than just once a quarter.

That ability to replan can fuel innovation in your organization. That's because the replanning can help you reassess the kind of work the organization does.

8.4 Use Value to Assess Your Work

There are three kinds of projects:

1. KTLO: Keep The Lights On projects: work you do to sustain the organization.
2. Grow: Grow the current business: extending the current products and services.
3. Transform: Possibly transformational projects.

You can estimate the Keep The Lights On work—often pretty well. You might be able to estimate the grow-the-current-business work. The possibly transformational work? No, you can't *easily* estimate that work.

If you want innovation, where should you invest your time? Innovative organizations spend more time in the last two buckets— the grow the current business and the possibly transformational work.

If you use estimation to plan, the Grow and Transform projects look quite risky. You might be tempted to spend most of your time in the KTLO projects.

However, if you use value to plan your time investment, you can change the work much more often. And, you might surprise yourself with areas you didn't think had possibilities—but do.

8.5 Options to Move to Value-Based Planning

I find value-based planning works best for me. However, I might not have convinced you yet. In that case, first, gather this data:

1. Add all the time your teams spend estimating their work in preparation for your portfolio planning. Remember, if they spend a week estimating every quarter, they're not delivering anything that week. When I've worked with clients, the managers and the teams regularly spend the last month of the quarter preparing backlogs and estimates for the next quarter. And, they spend time each week estimating what they will finish next. I've seen too many teams re-estimate their day's work at the start of a day. Too many organizations spend about one-quarter to one-third of their time estimating, not delivering.

2. How often do the teams adjust their forecast? Do the teams hit their estimations, every quarter? Since I've never seen that, I wonder how the teams can hit their forecasts every quarter. Or, do they adjust their forecast based on small, recent work so they can let you know what they can and cannot deliver?

3. How often would you like to change the project portfolio? Do the teams finish work as often as you would like? How often can the teams deliver work and how frequently do you want to change the project portfolio?

Now that you have data, ask yourself these questions:

1. If you want to plan work using value, who else do you need to enlist to attempt this change?

2. How will you enlist those people?
3. How long an experiment will you plan and what data will you show to assess that experiment?

I use cycle time as the basis for my short-range estimates, as I explained for the driving example. I use forecasts with ranges for longer-range planning. And, when I want to finish work, I evaluate by value to plan and deliver.

I encourage you to consider value for planning, regardless of what you're planning: a project, a product roadmap, or the project portfolio.

CHAPTER 9

Must We Utilize Everyone at 100%?

Back in the 1980s, I was a software developer. My boss asked me to spend 50% of my time on Project A, 35% of my time on Project B, and 15% of my time on Project C.

I sarcastically asked, "Should I work on Project D in my spare time?"

He didn't hear the sarcasm—or maybe he thought I would work a ton of overtime—and said, "Yes!"

I explained to him that 15% of my time was six hours a week. Given the context switching, I would be lucky to actually think for two hours on that project in a given week. I told him he could only pick two projects. What did he want me to work on?

He sighed and said, "Projects A and B." Not perfect, but a whole lot better.

9.1 Myth: 100% Utilization Works

A manager took me aside at a recent engagement. "You know, Johanna, there's something I just don't understand about this agile thing. It sure doesn't look like everyone is being used at 100 percent."

"And what if they aren't being used at 100 percent? Is that a problem for you?"

"Heck, yes. I'm paying their salaries! I want to know I'm getting their full value for what I'm paying them!"

"What if I told you you were probably getting *more* value than you're paying for, maybe one and a half to two times as much? Would you be happy with that?"

"Of course I'd be happy!" But, he asked, "How do you know that?"

I smiled, and said, "That's a conversation about cycle time and flow efficiency."

When I ask managers why they believe in this myth, they often tell me they think the teams can determine their work in advance. (See Which Teams Are the Best? on page 53 to see a little about how we all need to adapt to our work.) Because they don't realize how much technical people adapt, managers think that full utilization means they spend the company's money effectively.

The managers forget people need slack time for innovation, for serendipitous thinking, and to explore—never mind to adapt to the current reality.

Worse, there's gridlock. With 100 percent utilization, the very people you need on one project are already committed to one or more other projects. You can't get together for a meeting. You can't have a phone call. You can't even respond to email in a reasonable amount of time. Why? Because you're late responding to the other interrupts.

9.2 How Did We Get Here?

Back in the early days of computing, machines were orders of magnitude more expensive than programmers. In the 1970s, when I started working as a developer, companies could pay highly experienced programmers about $50,000 per year. You could pay those of us just out of school less than $15,000 per year, and we thought we were making huge sums of money.

In contrast, companies either rented machines for many multiples of tens of thousands of dollars per year or bought them for millions. Figure 9.1 visualizes how the scales of salaries to machine cost are not even close to equivalent.

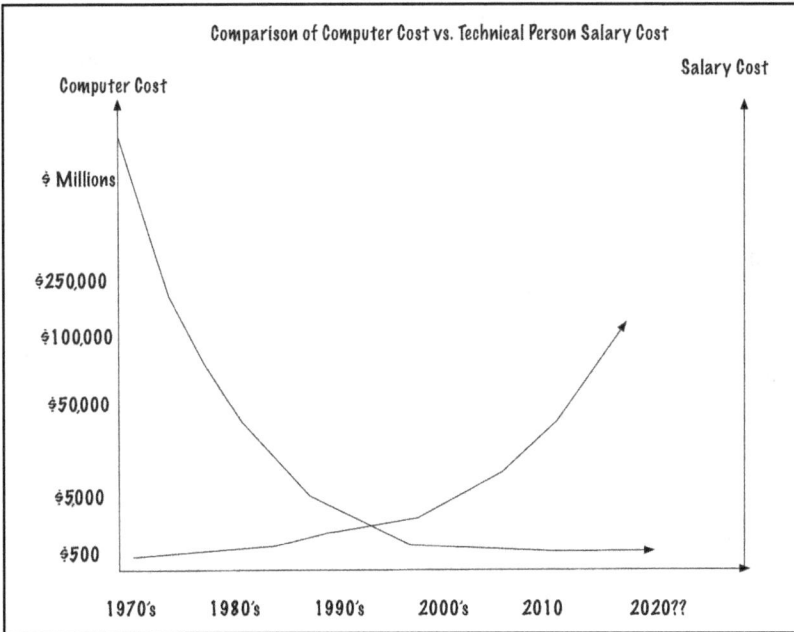

Figure 9.1: Computer Cost vs. Salary Cost

When computers were that expensive, we utilized every second of machine time—on one job at a time. We signed up for computer time. We desk-checked our work. We held design reviews and code reviews. We received *minutes* of computer time—yes, our jobs were often restricted to a minute of CPU time. If you wanted more time, you signed up for after-hours time, such as 2 A.M. to 4 A.M. When the machine time is scarce, we ask the machine to run all the time, one job at a time.

Realize that computer time was not the only expensive part of computing. Memory was expensive. Back in the old days, we had 256 bytes of memory and programmed in assembly language code. We had one page of code. If you had a routine that was longer than one page, you branched at the end of a page to another page that had room, and you had to swap it in. (Yes, often by hand. And, no, I am not nostalgic for the old days at all!)

In the late '70s and the '80s, minicomputers helped bring the scales of salary and computer price closer together. But it wasn't until minicomputers really came down in price and PCs started to dominate the market that the cost of a product developer became so much higher than the price of a computer.

With PCs, many people thought it was cheaper for a developer to spend time one-on-one with the computer, not in design reviews or in code/test reviews, or discussing the architecture with others.

In the '90s, even as the prices of computers, disks, and memory fell, and as programmers and testers became more expensive, it was clear to some of us that software development was more collaborative than just a developer one-on-one with his computer.

That's why Watts Humphrey and the Software Engineering Institute gained such traction during the '90s. Not because people liked heavyweight processes, but because, especially with a serial lifecycle, you had to do something to make product development more successful. And, many managers were stuck in 100 percent utilization thinking. Remember, it hadn't been that long since 100 percent utilization meant something—to the machine.

Now, remember what it means for a computer to be fully utilized, especially if it's a single-process machine: It can do only one thing at a time. It can't service any interrupts. It can't respond to any keystrokes. It can't update its status. It can only keep processing until it's done. That's what 100% utilization meant back in the '70s. We managed the WIP for the machine by only asking the machine to do one job at a time.

Now, let's assume the program behaves well and does not run in an infinite loop. The program finishes and the machine is ready for the next program/job. And, as soon as you add another simultaneous job or a user to the machine, the machine "splits" its memory and disk space to accommodate more simultaneous jobs.

And that's what we have with modern computers. Modern computers are multi-threaded, multi-process machines. The more simultaneous threads and processes, the more utilization the computer undergoes. If you've heard your machine's fan, or if you've seen your machine's processes thrash, your machine is in gridlock. That's the problem of 100% utilization.

Even if you haven't seen a machine under gridlock, I bet you've seen a highway at rush hour with no one moving. That's a highway at 100 percent utilization—it's a parking lot. Total gridlock.

We don't want highways at 100 percent utilization. We don't want current computers at 100 percent utilization either. If your computer gets to about 50 to 75 percent utilization, it feels slow. And, computers utilized at higher than 85 percent have unpredictable performance. Their throughput is unpredictable, and you can't tell what's going to happen. You can't tell when any of the processes will finish.

Unfortunately, people have precisely the same problem.

9.3 Why 100% Utilization Doesn't Work for People

Now, think of a human being. When we are at 100 percent utilization, we have no slack time at all. We run from one task or interrupt to another, not thinking. There are at least two things wrong with this picture: the inevitable attempt at multitasking and the not thinking.

We don't actually multitask at all; we fast-switch. When computers fast-switch, they write a perfect copy of what's in memory to disk and read that back in again when it's time to swap tasks. Because we are human, we are unable to perfectly write out what's in our memory, and we imperfectly swap back in what we've "written." So, there is a context-switch cost in the swapping, because we have to remember what we were thinking when we swapped out. And that takes time.

In addition, we experience a context switch in the time it takes us to swap out and swap back in. All of that time and imperfection adds up. And, because we are human, we do not perfectly allocate our time first to one task and then to another. If we have three tasks, we don't allocate 33 percent to each; we spend as much time as we please on each—*assuming* we want to spend 33 percent on each.

Let me address the not-thinking part of 100 percent utilization. What if you want people to consider working in a new way or learn something new? If you schedule or ask them to work at 100 percent utilization, will they try or learn? Not a chance. They can't consider it; they have no time.

The result is that people perform their jobs by rote, servicing their interrupts in the best way they already know, doing as little as possible, doing enough to get by. They cannot think of ways to improve. They cannot think of ways to help others. They cannot think of ways to innovate. They don't have the time.

They only think, "How the heck can I get out from under this mountain of work?" It's horrible for them, for the product, and for everyone they encounter.

When you ask people to work at 100 percent utilization, you get much less work out of them than when you plan for them to perform roughly four to six hours of technical work a day.

Here's how I came to the four to six hours of technical work a day: Let's assume everyone arrives at work at 8:30 A.M. and leaves at 5:30 P.M. and takes one hour for lunch. Let's also assume everyone drinks two coffees and takes a total of five bio-breaks during the day. And, let's assume everyone spends just one hour on email a day. (I addressed some of these issues in Book 2, starting in Chapter 1 where I explain how a culture of flow efficiency works better than a culture of resource efficiency.)

Before anyone gets to their work, they've spent 2.5 of their 9 hours on lunch, breaks, and emails. At maximum, they have 6.5 hours remaining in which to "work." The big question is how much time do people spend working and how much do they spend waiting? (See Book 2 and Visualize Your Team's Cycle Time on page 132 for how to measure that time.)

When you Encourage Flow Efficiency (page 12), the teams work together. They can ask and answer each other's questions. If people work alone, they tend to have more and longer wait times.

Let's take a look at a day of work. I normally plan for a chunk of work in the morning and a couple of chunks of work in the afternoon. When I pair, swarm, or mob, I tire more quickly. I have concentrated hard, all day. Even when I work alone, if I maintain focus (work time), I'm tired by the end of the day. I've done my fair share of work.

When I measure the ratio of work time to wait time in organizations, I often discover that people can rarely get more than three hours of work completed in a day. Why? They have meetings where they have to wait for someone to show up 15 minutes late. They can't finish a decision at these meetings because they need to wait for approval from someone else. They wait for a question from someone who is too busy to reply promptly. The list goes on.

The busy-ness means everyone context-switches several times a day. They lose their state. All because they're supposed to be fully utilized.

If we plan for four to six hours of work in a day, people might be able to achieve that. They cannot achieve eight hours of work. And, if you measure your work, you might realize you only achieve three to four hours of work in a day.

If you plan on 100 percent utilization, you get much less done in the organization. You create a terrible environment for work. And, you create an environment of no innovation. That doesn't sound like a recipe for success, does it?

9.4 Agile and Lean Approaches Make the Myth Transparent

Agile and lean approaches don't make 100 percent utilization go away; they make the myth transparent. By making sure that all the work goes into a backlog, they help management and the teams see what everyone is supposed to be working on and how impossible that is. That's the good news.

Once everyone can visualize the work, you can decide what to do about it. Maybe some of that work is for later, not for the next week or two. That's great—that's how we manage the product roadmap.

Maybe some of the work is part of another project and should be postponed for another iteration. That's great—that's how we manage the project portfolio.

Maybe some of the work should be done by someone, but not by this team. That's great—that's an impediment that some manager can manage and fix.

No matter what you do, you can't do anything until you see the work. As long as you visualize the work in its entirety, you can manage it.

Remember, no one can do anything if they are 100 percent utilized. If you want to provide full value for your organization, you need to be "utilized" at about 50 to 60 percent. Because a mind, any mind, is a terrible thing to waste.

9.5 Can We Accommodate Fast Switching?

Your experience might indicate that you can fast-switch between your various management projects. It's true, you might be able to do so. That's because, as a manager, you have small deliverables between relatively long wait states.

Figure 9.2 on page 103 shows a value stream map from a blog post I wrote about a client with these problems[1]:

Knowledge workers work the other way: if you want them to work as fast as possible, they need to spend more time on focused thought and concentration—often with others. They need very short or nonexistent waits states—that is, interrupts to their focus.

---

[1] https://www.jrothman.com/mpd/2018/06/why-managers-believe-multitasking-works-long-decision-wait-times/

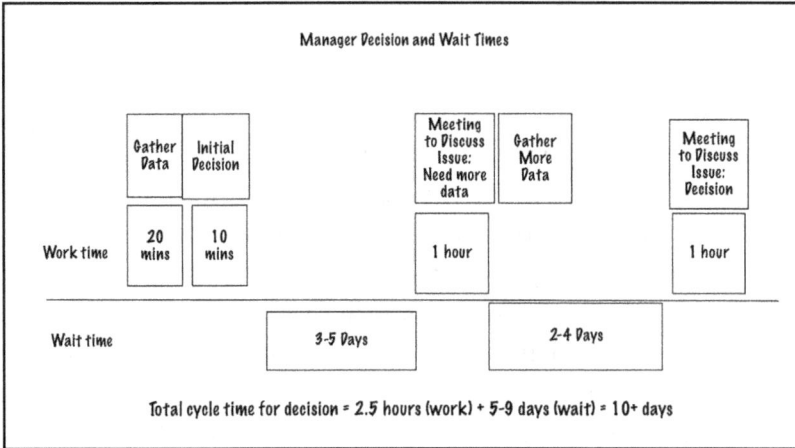

Figure 9.2: Cycle time for manager decisions

When you fast-switch, you're done with that work *for now*. When knowledge workers fast-switch, they lose context. They pay the price to regain their context when they try to delve into the work again.

People need to focus to finish work.

9.6 Options to Avoid 100% Utilization

If you want to avoid 100% utilization, you'll learn to Say No (page 112) to some work. That No will allow you to say Yes to other work.

If you can't say no, you're never able to say yes.

You have options. You'll need thinking time to consider your options. You might multitask so much that you feel as if you don't have time to think. Do take the time. You will discover you have more work time in your day when you do.

One hundred percent utilization doesn't work for highways, or computers, and definitely not for people. That means you'll need to learn how to say no to more work. If you need to report utilization, ask this question:

What will the person asking for this information do with it?
Can I report different information that might offer more value?

Utilization doesn't make sense, because we can't plan for unplanned work. If we don't have slack in the system, we can't manage the production support issues or the emergencies that arise.

1. Make sure everyone on a team is on the same project and only that project. Do not expect teams to work on even two projects at one time. If you think you need a team to work on multiple projects, reduce the time the team spends on any one project and then have them change to the other project. The team can finish more work when they focus on one project at a time.

2. Make sure the team understands the purpose of the project and its expected outcomes, not just the tasks someone wants to assign to them.

3. Flow work through teams as a way to Encourage Flow Efficiency on page 12. If a team has not collaborated before, you might have to train them to work together. (See Training Is a Necessary Part of Knowledge Work on page 122 to help people practice how to collaborate.)

4. Ask the team to deliver very small chunks of value, something a customer can use, as often as possible. I like teams to deliver a small story every day. The more often they deliver something of value, the less pressure everyone feels and the more often you can change the project portfolio.

5. Learn how to say No in several forms: "What should I stop doing?", "Not now." "Here are the risks." For more specifics, see *Manage Your Project Portfolio: Increase Your Capacity and Finish More Projects, 2nd ed* [ROT16].

6. Ask teams to map their value stream to see where they have wait states. Then, learn the reason for any wait states. The team might need you to help solve the problem of wait states.

If you currently work in an environment where utilization thinking reigns, you might need to show various people anonymous value stream maps from teams. Anonymize those maps so the managers can't blame anyone. Flow efficiency is not obvious to many managers. Help them see the reality that 100% utilization makes everything take longer.

CHAPTER 10

Can't I Move People From Project to Project?

If you want an innovative organization, you might think you need to change what people do—every time someone requests a change.

Several years ago, a senior manager at a client organization took me aside and said, "Agile costs too much. It breaks our shared services model."

I asked the manager to tell me more.

"We used to be able to save money because we had a pool of testers, of UI people, of writers. Everything except developers. Those, we had to keep on certain teams. But, we could shift people wherever and whenever we needed when we used shared services."

I nodded. "Yup, that sounds right."

"Now," he said, "We need whole teams. We can't use shared services. We need to fund teams, not projects." He shook his head. "Everything costs more."

"Really?" I asked. "My experience is that the actual projects, the time to first and ongoing deliverables, costs less."

"Yes, of course, that costs less," he said. "But, we don't have people working on everything, all the time. We have to choose what people work on. We don't have shared services anymore. We have project teams."

"And, the problem is?" I asked.

"We need more teams if we want to fund and then finish all that work," he said. "We can't."

I nodded. "Exactly. You're not tricking yourself into thinking you *can* fund everything. Now you know you can't. You know you have to decide what's most important now and what you can fund later." I paused. "I'd say your agile approaches are working. You might not like what you see, but what you see is now accurate."

"Where will I find the money?" he asked.

"If your products return the revenue you want, you should be able to recognize product and support revenue earlier. And, if you really want, you can capitalize the work earlier."

He nodded. "Fine," he said. "But we need to change what the teams do more quickly than they can deliver."

"That's a different problem," I said. "We can review the various delays inside and between teams, and how long it takes to decide before the teams get the work. And, we can discuss how to help the product people change from 'we need everything' thinking to 'how little they can do' and still release value. The product folks might not be thinking about how to define product experiments and minimums. But, the shared services model never really worked. It just hid the real costs and delays."

He nodded. "Okay, you're right."

When managers manage the project portfolio—and ask teams to collaborate on the work—the entire organization sees benefits.

10.1 Myth: I Can Move People Like Chess Pieces

Ben appeared at the entrance to Sally's cube. "Sally, I need you to stop testing on this project and move over to Dan's project." He turned to leave.

"Not so fast, Ben," Sally said.

He turned around and faced her.

"Are you serious? I just started this project a month ago. I just started to learn what's going on. I finally have the trust of the team. I haven't worked with these guys before. I found a nice, juicy bug last week and proved my value to the team. Why would you ask me to move now?"

Ben sat in her visitor's chair. "I need to staff Dan's project with testers and you are my only available tester."

"I'm not available! What are you going to do in a month? Move me back here? Heck no, I won't go. No." Sally thought for a few seconds.

Ben shook his head and opened his mouth.

Sally held up her hand. "Wait a minute. You're always going on about the project portfolio. So, which project is more important? This one, or Dan's project?"

Ben tapped his pen. "Well, this one. But Dan really wants a tester, and you're so good. I wanted to put someone good on his project."

Sally brightened and said, "OK, this is easy. Just tell him you don't have anyone. I'm your most senior tester, and I can tell you that you don't have anyone. Look at our project portfolio posted on the wall. Everyone is assigned for the next two months, the next four iterations. Are you managers going to change the project portfolio before then?"

Ben sighed. "No, we aren't."

"Well then, what's the problem? You just tell Dan, 'No.' That's not so hard, is it?"

"Well, it is. I hate to disappoint people," Ben said.

Sally laughed. "Ah, that's the problem," she said. "You want to be a nice guy. Well, tough. You're a manager now. You don't get to be a nice guy all the time. You have to take a stand. You negotiate with people at the project portfolio meeting, right?"

"Yes, I do."

"And you go back and forth and horse-trade, right? You make the tough decisions about which projects are most important, right? You decide which projects to staff and not staff, right?"

"Yes, I do."

"And did you tell Dan at the most recent project portfolio meeting that you didn't have any testers?"

"Yes, I did."

"So, why is he bugging you now? Did he think you magically conjured some more testers out of thin air? Now, that would be a good trick."

"Well, I think he was hoping my priorities would have changed."

"Have they?"

"No. They follow the corporate project portfolio."

"Well, tell Dan the magic word, 'No.' Nicely, of course," Sally said and grinned.

"But he needs testers."

"Of course he does. He has developers. They'll have to take the place of testers. Or he shouldn't have started the project. But that's not your problem. Did you explain to everyone what would happen if they started a project without testers?"

"Of course I did!"

"So Dan only has himself to blame," Sally said. "Look, the buck stops with you."

Ben sighed and shook his head.

Sally continued. "Your job as a manager is to protect us from being moved around like chess pieces. You and I have had this conversation before. In fact, we had it just last month, and the month before that."

Ben nodded. "You're right."

Sally said, "It's not about me being right. Even when we collaborate, it takes time for people to build solution-space domain expertise. When I get pulled off a project and put on another one, I can't become a part of the team. I don't learn the product adequately. It doesn't matter if we're talking about testers or developers or business analysts—if that person doesn't know the risks, the idiosyncrasies of the people, or the product, the team can't be successful."

Ben looked down at his notebook and sighed.

"So, what are you going to do, Ben?"

"I'm going to tell Dan no—and nicely." Ben smiled.

Sally laughed. "Excellent. I'll go back to testing now and see what other evil bugs I can find."

10.2 Managers Can't Please Everyone

It's impossible to please everyone in the organization. Other organizational leaders will come to you with what appear to be reasonable requests. If that request is about moving a tester or a developer to a different project, examine whether the request is actually reasonable.

If you want to lead for innovation and change, ask yourself these questions:

- What does the person want, for both their work and the team they want to be a part of?
- Does the requested work rank higher than the project this person works on now?
- Should this person's entire team move to the new project, to help it finish faster?

You can't optimize for innovation and change unless the people finish work so they can move to the next chunk of work. And, you can't optimize for innovation unless people work in flow efficiency.

Your Position Amplifies Your Comments

Sometimes, managers—especially senior managers—don't realize the power of their questions or comments.

The CEO, Janet, loved to wander around, asking questions of the Engineering teams. On almost every walk, Dan, Janet's administrative assistant, took notes.

Janet would ask questions, such as, "What's your data strategy?" or "Have you considered this alternative architecture?"

As Janet moved to the next team, Dan said, "Don't change what you're doing. She's curious, not asking for changes."

Janet brought Dan on his walks so he could "sweep up" after her. She'd learned that one of her curious questions might trigger a team to head in a different direction. Even if she told people not to change direction, they might anyway. Dan helped the teams understand they should stick with the current project portfolio.

The more senior your position, the more your comments might cause a team to change direction. You might not anticipate how people will respond to your off-the-cuff comments.

Learn to say no.

10.3 Say No

The most important word in a manager's arsenal is the word "No." Use the word No when people ask you for any number of not-so-useful actions:

- Requests that will hurt someone else, either physically or emotionally.
- Requests that don't fit reasonable guidelines and constraints—or you can't figure out a way to make their request fit.
- Requests for you to take on more work than you or your teams are supposed to deliver.

You have many ways to say No. (See *Manage Your Project Portfolio: Increase Your Capacity and Finish More Projects, 2nd ed* [ROT16] for examples.) I've found these questions and statements useful:

- "What should we stop doing?"
- "No, we don't have more capacity," and show the person your portfolio.
- "I see the following risks if we attempt to do more work."

Not every manager can say No with a straight face. Too often, the manager feels compelled by the requestor's position in the organization.

If you have trouble with the word No, use this simulation to learn to say No:

1. Gather six to twenty people together in one room. If you can, do this with a management team that's larger than three people. More people makes this simulation work better.
2. Set a timer for 45 seconds. Ask everyone to walk around the room and say the word "Yes" to everyone they see. At the end of the time, everyone stops where they are.
3. Set a timer for 45 seconds. Now, as people walk around the room, say the word "No" to everyone. At the end of the time, everyone stops.
4. Set a timer for 45 seconds. Now, people choose what to say: either Yes or No. They can choose for each person they see.

At the end, debrief with these questions for everyone who spoke. Make sure you offer people enough time to think and then speak:

- What did it feel like to say Yes at the start?
- What did it feel like to say No?
- What did it feel like to choose?
- What did you learn from your experience?
- What might you do next?

Make sure you can say No.

If you use transparency to visualize all the work, people start to understand how much work you can do and what you can't do.

10.4 Visualize the Work at All Levels

In *Manage Your Project Portfolio: Increase Your Capacity and Finish More Projects, 2nd ed* [ROT16], I suggested you might need to use a variety of lenses to see the project portfolio in ways that fit your needs.

I recommend a calendar view, several possible kanban visualizations, and sometimes, you'll need to see the variety of project types in the portfolio.

If you don't have an easy way to visualize all the work, you can't say No. You can't help other people see the system of work.

I do recommend you create portfolios at all levels, with the requisite detail. For example, at the highest level, the senior managers create a portfolio that addresses the various objectives. At the lowest level, a team would visualize their project portfolio. And, the middle managers might create more visualizations to see where they might need to create experiments and when to stop work if there's no more value in that project.

Don't forget to include the unstaffed work somewhere. I prefer to park that work, but some organizations don't like using parking lots. If your organization wants to maintain the illusion that all the work is on a list somewhere, create an unstaffed column or row. Do not include the unstaffed work in the visualization of the actual work. Separate it somehow.

Set other people's expectations about the work that's in progress and the work that's not in progress. And, see if you can't start parking work that you can't start now.

When you visualize all the work at all the various levels, including the unstaffed work, everyone is more likely to avoid asking anyone to do work they can't do. And, everyone is more likely to flow work through teams.

10.5 Flow Projects Through Teams

When you flow work through teams, you reinforce flow efficiency over resource efficiency at the team level. Even better, you can reinforce *management* flow efficiency—because the managers focus on the same few objectives.

Do Teams Have to Stay Together Forever?

You might wonder if you should keep teams together forever. No, and that's because teams can get "stale" or rigid if they stay together for too long. (See *Dynamic Reteaming: The Art and Wisdom of Changing Teams* [HEL19] for more details.)

Inviting a team to change and offering changes to people differs from imposing a new person on a team. In addition, reteaming is about the team as a unit, not about an individual.

And, you don't have the problem of shared services, or of managers asking for particular people to join specific teams "just for a while." You'll also see where you don't have complete teams.

When you see where you're missing people needed to make complete cross-functional teams, you can choose what to do and when to do it.

10.6 Capitalize on Each Person's Individualities

People are not chess pieces—we are not fungible. Everyone brings different strengths, capabilities, and perspectives to a project team.

If you're wondering how to create teams, you don't have to. You can ask people to self-organize into teams. See *Creating Great Teams: How Self-Selection Lets People Excel* [MAM15] for ideas to help people choose their teams. And, if you have component teams and you really don't think you can change to cross-functional teams, consider reading *Rethinking Component Teams for Flow*[1] to flow work through the scarce people.

---

[1] https://www.jrothman.com/mpd/portfolio-management/2017/01/rethinking-component-teams-for-flow/

Instead of treating people as if they are chess pieces, treat them as the unique individuals they are and you will gain much more from your teams.

10.7 Options to Collaborate on the Project Portfolio

I've seen several root causes for the problem of managers moving people from project to project.

- Sometimes, the organization created single-component or single-function teams. Those teams need to collaborate with other teams to create a product that the organization can release.
- Sometimes, the managers believe in resource efficiency rather than flow efficiency.
- Sometimes, the managers don't realize they need to collaborate on the project portfolio.

In my experience (which might not be your experience), all three of these problems are a result of reward structures. The rewards drive each manager to focus on *their* objectives, not the overarching organizational objectives.

Each manager—and all the managers—are subject to Lewin's equation, described in Environment Shapes Everyone's Behavior on page 10.

I would love it if organizations actually started with the reward structure. However, I'm not that naive. You can start with a single project portfolio that matches the company's objectives—and reinforces the rewards.

Start here:

1. Clarify the organization's customers and objectives to create more satisfied customers.
2. Gather all the work across the organization. How much of that work aligns with the current objectives? You don't have to

consider any work that does not align with *current* objectives. You can put all the other work in the Parking Lot. And, tell the senior managers which work is in the parking lot.

3. If you see work that doesn't *appear* to align with the organization's objectives, ask questions. There might be other or hidden objectives you don't know about. I've seen plenty of projects that various people instigated to help their resumes.

4. As a management team, decide together which teams will work on which projects. Fund the teams. Make sure the teams can deliver something useful before you need to evaluate the project portfolio again.

See *Manage Your Project Portfolio: Increase Your Capacity and Finish More Projects, 2nd ed* [ROT16] for more details.

You don't have to move people around to finish work.

When you manage your project portfolio, you'll see which projects need teams and which ones don't for now. When teams finish work, you can change the work or change the teams, or both. You'll achieve better cycle time, lead time, and flow efficiency. All of these result in delivering better work to the customers faster which will increase your revenue.

CHAPTER 11

Don't People Already Know How to Do Their Jobs?

Many managers believe that they should be able to hire people who already have all the technical and interpersonal skills necessary. Or, that people should be able to learn on their own time and bring that knowledge to work. Or, that people learned everything they needed to learn in school.

When I was a new manager, I fell for this myth. Oh, I knew enough to make sure that we had team-based learning. I knew enough to make sure we learned from people inside the organization. I knew enough to buy books.

But conferences or on-site training? I learned the hard way.

Amy, a tester, told me we were too insular with our testing. Amy persuaded me to find the money and send her to a conference for a week. She was right. She returned with so many ideas we needed six months to experiment with all of them. We tested faster and better. Her trip paid for itself within a month.

Later, I worked as a manager, where the VP brought a variety of training into my organization for technical staff: specific programming languages, hiring, and influence workshops.

We learned and practiced—on our specific products, and with our colleagues. We used our context to learn. We were able to recoup our investment in training, often inside of a few weeks. Yes, we could point to time saved or faster development because of those workshops inside of a month.

As a consultant, I've offered technical and managerial workshops. Every client tells me they gained significant learning during the workshop, and the workshop pays for itself in just a few weeks.

Not every workshop or conference is right for you. The quality of the learning environment matters. However, I've learned in sessions and in the hallway conversations between sessions. As a side benefit, I've built my network at workshops and conferences. Then, when my problems stymied me, I knew people I could ask for help.

You might think workshops or conferences are expensive. They are only expensive if you don't use the learning you acquired there.

11.1 Myth: We Have No Time for Training

"Hey, George, I want to talk to you about training for my group," Lakshmi said.

"Don't start with that again," George said. "I know you have a group of developers who need training. Two years ago, when you ran testing, you had a group of testers who needed training. Why do all your groups need training?"

"Everyone needs training. Even you and I need training," Lakshmi persisted.

"I don't need training. I listen to books on tape—abridged books, at that. I get everything I need in my abridged books. I only have to spend seven minutes on a book while I drive."

"Hold it right there," Lakshmi said. "You listen to abridged summaries of business books? On your drive into work? No wonder you didn't understand my argument last week against forced ranking. You need to listen to books all the way through, my friend. You are missing significant pieces."

George frowned.

"But let's get back to my problem," Lakshmi said. "I have a big list of training wants. I want everyone to learn functional programming because that new product is going to use that approach."

"Now we're talking," George said.

"That's not the end of my list," Lakshmi said. "I also want to bring in workshops for hiring and influence skills. I had workshops in my previous job, and you're always telling me that you like the fact I hire quickly. And, that you and I agree on many issues—eventually."

"Well, I do like the fast hiring," George said. "I didn't realize you influenced me."

Lakshmi smiled. "Yup, I do. Even when we don't agree the first time, we explore options so we can find some middle ground that serves us both."

George grinned. "Yes, you do that. I see that now." He paused. "But do the engineers need these workshops, too? Maybe just the managers."

Lakshmi thought for a moment. "I took these workshops when I was an engineer. I've gotten better through practice and coaching from my managers. That's how I became so good at these skills."

"What's wrong with the way the engineers hire now?"

Lakshmi started ticking reasons off on her fingers. "They don't always ask the right kinds of questions about their particular topic. And the follow-up meeting after the interview? We still have problems when the person with the loudest opinion thinks he or she will win the discussion."

"You're not going to tell me who the loudest person is, are you?"

"Not at all," Lakshmi said.

George said, "Huh. We need to know we're hiring the best people for the job. That's a big deal."

"I know exactly the books and workshops I need, and I know when I want to bring them in. I want to start with a book study group to set the stage. I don't want everyone to go into the training cold. I want to challenge the trainers. We have really sharp people, and I want to turn them loose on these problems."

George said, "What if we just had a book study group?"

Lakshmi sighed and shook her head. "I can create that group. And, I can facilitate the discussions. However, I don't think I can create the practice in the study group. I'm not the right person to offer feedback or coaching on how people do the practice. And, most importantly, people need specific time to practice."

"I don't know," George said. "Seems like a lot of work for you and greater expense than I considered for me. Not just for the training, but for the time we take from the project work." He paused. "And, what if we train them and they leave?" George said.

"George, what if we *don't* train them and they stay?"

George sighed and said, "I see your point. Let me think about it a little more."

"I'll check in with you next week," Lakshmi said. "Maybe I can influence you to yes by then."

11.2 Training Is a Necessary Part of Knowledge Work

It's never easy to schedule training. It always seems to interfere with "real" work—project work. But, if you want people to learn a new language, a new tool, or a new skill, for instance, an interpersonal skill such as Lakshmi described, then you need to create training time. I like to schedule training time every single week.

When I served a single-function team (testers or developers), I scheduled an hour of training each week. We met weekly as a functional group to solve problems together or learn together. (We didn't have status meetings.)

We generated a backlog of topics we wanted to discuss or learn. We rank-ordered the topics. Each person took responsibility for one topic. That person either recruited a person to explain the topic or explained it to the rest of the team.

When I served managers, I asked the team how they wanted to learn. In addition to bringing in training, we read books and discussed them for an hour each week.

Here are other approaches I've seen work:

- Create a book club that meets at a specific time each week. Choose (and buy) a book for all the participants.
- Create communities of practice that meet each week. If you're not already using communities of practice, consider how you serve the communities to structure their work and how they invite people to participate. As a manager, you can ask them to tell you when they need any information or money. You might want to check in every so often and see if they need external training.
- As a last resort, consider a lunch-and-learn. I hesitate to ask people to relinquish their lunchtime. Lunch is outside of work time.

For technical teams, consider mob programming and coding katas. I think of these practices as invitations to the team. Not all teams use mobbing or katas as a regular team practice.

Every so often, at least once a quarter, review the learning opportunities. I like to ask people, "Is there something you want to learn?" They will tell you.

If you are worried about the frequency of imposing learning on people, ask them if the training frequency is too high. They will tell you.

Sometimes, people appear to not want training. In my experience, people don't want training if they think they already know something, or if they feel too much pressure to deliver. Or, if they believe the people providing the training are incompetent.

Discover why people don't want training and address that problem.

The longer you make the break between learning opportunities, the more difficult the learning is to restart. And, the more likely you are to stop learning and training entirely.

It's easier on your schedule to learn a little every week rather than have a huge hit once every six months. Some of my clients say, "Stopping work for three days to learn in a workshop costs us so much time." They say this even when they realize that what they will learn will save them at least a day that week and a day the following week.

If you feel as if you can't take time for training, that's precisely the time you need training. Something is wrong with the way work is flowing, or rather, not flowing, through the organization.

Instead, if you have some form of team/group learning for an hour or less each week, the training time is unnoticeable for the project but adds up for the people.

11.3 Make Time for Conferences, Too

Every so often, you need an injection of a wide variety of new ideas from many new people. That means it's time for a conference. If you're lucky enough to find a local conference, you won't have to incur travel costs. And, many conferences offer a virtual option or are totally virtual.

Look for user groups, agile, open space, and professional group conferences. Yes, the quality of the conferences varies. Consider exploring who has extensive experience and has the capacity to help other people learn from that experience. Not all well-known people are great speakers or session leaders.

But, no matter what kind of sessions you find at a conference, one of the best things conferences offer is networking. I find that when I meet people in or out of my sessions, we all learn a lot. What we learn can be different from the objectives of the formal talks and tutorials.

When you network to find other people with similar problems, you learn not only how they have solved their problems but also what didn't work for them. You can learn from their experiments and experiences, trade notes, and, depending on your geographic location, possibly exchange job candidates or hiring tips.

Because you are face-to-face at a conference, you can learn more when you network than you can by email or any other electronic forum. If you have not been to a conference in a while, consider going to a local conference this year. Then, depending on your budget, set aside time and budget for a national or international conference. In many cases, speakers attend for free—your only costs are travel. I learn about culture and practices from my international colleagues, and both my international and domestic clients benefit from what I learn.

11.4 Capitalize on Curiosity

Many knowledge workers are curious. Use that curiosity to build in training as a weekly endeavor. You won't be sorry. Yes, training can be expensive. In my experience, the value of the training significantly outweighs the cost.

But, what's the cost if you don't train people and they stay?

11.5 Evidence That People Need Training

Maybe you're not sure people need training. Ask yourself these questions:

- Have you had a difficult time hiring people with the "right" skills? You might be looking for skills you can train—and skills people can learn in context, on the job.
- Do people need a different mental model from which to view their work? Sometimes, people go to a conference, listen to a speaker, or talk to someone in the hallway, and they reframe how they think about their work.
- Do people need other practical knowledge they can adapt from someone else's experience? They might rethink how they work based on experiences they hear about at a conference.

When people start to see their work differently, they can create experiments with their team. They will gain valuable learning, regardless of any experiment's results.

Watch to make sure people feel as if they have time to experiment. It won't matter if you offer training if people feel as if they don't have the time to learn something new.

11.6 **Options for Training**

You do need to spend some time or money on training. However, you don't need to spend a fortune.

1. The cheap and easy way to start training is to conduct a weekly learning session with a team. I've asked the team to decide on a specific time during the week to learn. Then, I ask the team to brainstorm a list of topics they want to learn. They rank all the items, and it's either my job or the job of a "learning coordinator" to find people to lead these topics. Each team member spends a month as the learning coordinator. They then hand off the role to the next person. This way, no one feels the burden for too long.

2. Buy books that people want. Consider a weekly book discussion group. Regardless of whether people attend, buy everyone a book. Their book, not the company's book. You don't know when they might read it. Some people like to write in the margins. Buy a copy for the company library, too. That way, when you hire new people, they can read the book. And, if the book is really good, buy a copy of the book for all new hires.

3. Investigate conferences where you or people you serve can speak. Speakers often receive free entry into conferences. People can practice their public speaking skills, which is another form of learning. When you have to explain something, you tend to learn it in even more depth.

Consider asking people what they want for training. They will tell you.

CHAPTER 12

Doesn't Lower Salaries Mean Lower Project Cost?

For my entire career in software product development, my managers and my clients have endured substantial pressure to reduce costs. One approach is hiring lower-salaried people to get the work done faster—to take advantage of their lower costs.

Back in the early 2000s, I consulted with a Boston-based organization that had a lot of what they called "commodity" work. The CIO outsourced that commodity work to India. Unfortunately, the work wasn't quite commodity work—it supported the main product development work. The communication delays and the tools available at that time overwhelmed the ability of either the Boston team or the India team to work effectively.

When I asked the CIO why he outsourced that work, he said, "I have to bring the cost of our product development down. We can't make enough money with our current business model to pay for the people we need."

Later, in the late-2000s, I facilitated a retrospective for a large Engineering organization. They had several hundred people in one facility in the Boston area. In addition, they employed key contributors and teams across Asia and Europe.

Given the specialized knowledge the teams needed, the VP of this organization knew he had already recruited most of the suitable available people in the Boston area. "I need to be able to hire smart people anywhere in the world," he said. "And, if I hire them where wages are lower than in the US, I should be able to realize substantial cost savings."

We conducted a retrospective that showed the VP he wasn't getting all the value he expected for the salaries he paid. "How can I spend so much money and get so little return?" He thought he'd adequately funded the people and the teams. He was sure he had the right people in the right places. Why did the work cost so much?

I've worked with other senior managers who wanted to save money on their work. Or, they didn't want to reduce the number of projects in the project portfolio. They had too many projects for the available teams.

Too many of these well-meaning managers also tried these actions:

- Hired testers in a lower-wage part of the world to save salary costs. This had the effect of reducing or eliminating collaboration time between the testers and the rest of the team.
- Tried to carve out products that the original team would transfer to the new offshored team. In my experience, too often, the new team still needed support from the original team.
- Hired developers in one location, testers in a second location, and product people in a third location. Each location was at least eight hours from the other location. This approach also reduced collaboration time.
- Tried "follow-the-sun," with handoffs as a way to maintain momentum.

Each of these ideas, including various techniques for outsourcing and offshoring, relies on just one lever to change the project cost: resource efficiency. (For more information about resource efficiency and flow efficiency, see *This is Lean: Resolving the Efficiency Paradox* [MOA13] or *The Principles of Product Development Flow: Second Generation Lean Product Development* [REI09]. I also wrote about the problems of resource efficiency thinking around teams in Book 2.)

The problem is that resource efficiency doesn't account for the delays between the people who need to work together. Those delays can cost significant *time*. You still pay people their salaries, even if they're waiting for an answer to a question. The longer people wait for an answer to their question, the more expensive that question is.

Resource efficiency thinking is particularly seductive if you think that the people in different locations across the world are independent. In my experience, it's quite difficult to create truly independent teams, especially if they work on the same product.

These managers struggled with the questions of how to fund product support activities, hire smart people outside of one geographic location, and create independent teams—all to save money.

You can save money—and project time—when you address cycle time, not individual wage costs. Cycle time helps you see the delays in communication that lead to a longer and more expensive project.

12.1 Myth: Lower Wages Mean Less Expensive Projects

"George is on his offshoring rampage again," Cindy, the QA Director, said as she slumped down in Ted's visitor chair.

Ted, the Development Director, saved his document and turned around. "Oh? Want to tell me about it?"

"I need more testers for the feature teams we're starting, right? I told him. I showed him the project portfolio and the projects we can't start. I *showed* him my unstaffed work. He told me, 'Hire people in India. They're cheaper.' Well, they are cheaper, but we have so many delays: the delays of bringing people up to speed, communication delays, and work delays where someone has a question and they don't get an answer fast enough."

Ted nodded. "Yup, I've seen that too."

"All those delays means the total project cost goes up," Cindy said. "And, the delays mean the wage savings don't make sense. The people are smart, really smart, but by the time we get them trained on the product, combined with the time delay, it's just not worth it."

Ted nodded. "I think we can offer him some alternatives."

Cindy continued, "Maybe," she said. "We're in Denver, so south is better than east. Mexico? Brazil? But why can't I just hire testers here? Are you getting pushback on hiring developers?"

"Yes," Ted agreed. "I'm being told to hire developers in Ukraine."

"Well, that's just crazy," Cindy said. "We don't have enough hours of overlap. We should hire complete feature teams somewhere. And make them employees. Doesn't George realize that?"

"He's still thinking in resource efficiency terms," Ted said. "You know—first you need developers, then you need testers. We have to help him see we need everyone all the time. We need to explain to him the cost of asking a question and the cost of delay waiting for an answer. Maybe we should show him the value stream."

"He wants all the advantages of agile without understanding the first thing about it. Even if we weren't agile, it wouldn't make sense to have people that far away."

Ted nodded. "Yup."

Cindy wasn't done yet. "We spend time developing requirements or a feature, then we have to send it to someplace more than eight hours away for testing? How do we explain to the poor testers what we mean? They don't have the context."

Ted nodded. "Right again."

"And, if they aren't employees, we get different people every month," Cindy said. "We keep training people, week after week. I swear, at my last company, I must have trained six people in a year. When I asked what happened to them, the answer from their management was, 'They left.' When I asked the testers, one finally told me, 'They got a better job for more money at a larger company.' We paid for their training."

Ted said, "I agree. That's my experience, too. The people aren't the problem. It's how we're supposed to work with them."

"I don't mind training people, but I want to hang on to them for more than eight weeks," Cindy said. "We have to make them employees. Or we need a good offshoring partner, not just some commodity body shop. The way George is going into this, he's going for the cheapest price. That's no way to run a business where we need speed."

Ted nodded.

"The delays on the project are going to cost way more than any labor cost would be," Cindy fumed.

"Have you written up any of your experiences with offshoring?"

"No."

"I've had some of the same experiences you've had. I've had great experiences with feature teams. I've had bad experiences with just developers or just testers. Let's explain our experiences to George and put some dollar values to those experiences. If we articulate why we're so frustrated and that we're not against feature teams in other places, maybe we can get George to listen to us."

"Okay. Let's write it together."

12.2 Project Cost Is More Than Wage Cost

Knowledge workers learn together as they create a product. Back in Create Career Ladders on page 47, I suggested the manager's role in performance management was to facilitate the team's ability to learn together. That means teams need enough hours of overlap to collaborate as a team.

In *From Chaos to Successful Distributed Agile Teams: Collaborate to Deliver* [ROK19], Mark Kilby and I recommend agile teams have a minimum of four hours of overlap to enable collaboration. We have not seen many teams with just two hours of overlap collaborate effectively. And teams with zero hours of overlap? Both of us too often see everyone finishing "their" work with no focus on the team's outcomes.

When the team has sufficient time to collaborate, it might not matter where people are. As I write this during the COVID-19 pandemic, many of us work from our homes. We are all dispersed. And, the teams that can agree on which hours of the day they will collaborate are the ones most effective at their work.

While salary is one component of project cost, the most effective lever for project cost is cycle time.

12.3 Visualize Your Team's Cycle Time

In Book 2, I suggested that the team learn how to measure their cycle time. If you want to reduce project cost and you're considering hiring or contracting with people at distance, consider creating a value stream map to see the *best* possible response time for the team's work.

Here's an example I've seen too often. A developer in the Eastern U.S. time zone works with a tester in India.

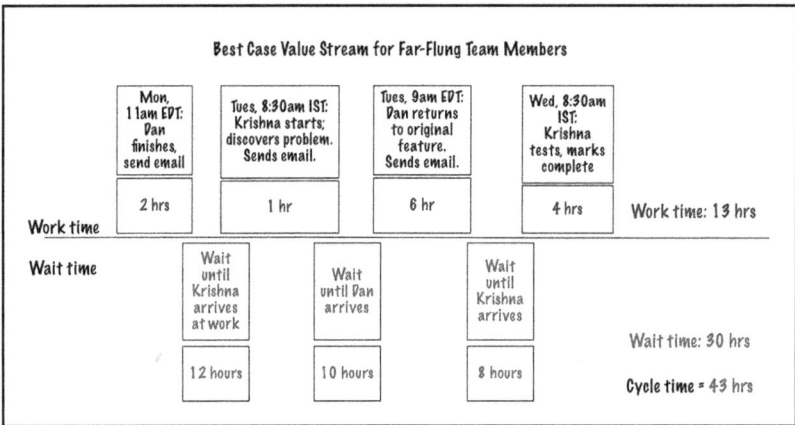

Figure 12.1: Value Stream for Far-Flung Team Members

Dan, the developer, finishes a feature at eleven o'clock on Monday morning EDT. Krishna learns Dan is done via email, or possibly a board notification. Krishna's time zone is 9.5 hours ahead of Dan, so Krishna has already left for the day when Dan finishes.

Krishna arrives at work the next morning and starts testing. Krishna finds something unexpected and notifies Dan.

However, Dan has already started a new feature. When Dan learns Krishna is stuck, Dan interrupts himself, causing a context switch.

Dan has choices. He can return to the feature he thought he completed. He can finish the new feature—speeding through it, so he can finish his current thinking. Whatever he chooses, Dan incurs an interruption.

These interruptions and context-switching make everything take longer—and increase the project cost. These are examples of times your far-flung team will incur longer cycle times:

- When people need to understand some specific item or issue.
- When it's time for the "next" person to work on the item.
- When someone made a mistake and the item must return for more development or more testing or more architecture.

When people don't have enough hours of overlap, and one person on the team needs to ask another person on the team a question, the entire team suffers that delay. That delay increases the cost of each feature.

In this case, where Dan needs almost a full day to rework the feature, the cycle time is 43 hours, and three full days. The work time was 13 hours—about two days of work.

You can create successful geographically distributed teams. For more information about how to make distributed agile teams successful, see *From Chaos to Successful Distributed Agile Teams: Collaborate to Deliver* [ROK19].

If you're considering moving work to a lower-salary location, create a value stream map of what occurs in a team now—and include the time zone effects. Understand the cost of delay when people don't work where they can easily collaborate.

12.4 Cost of Delay Affects Any Project, Agile or Not

I've used developers and testers as the examples here, but you might have the developers and testers together and while the product management is remote. I've seen Scrum Masters who were remote from their teams—something I don't understand at all.

Any time you have a necessary role with insufficient hours of overlap with others on the team, you incur delays in the project. Those delays increase the overall project cost.

Maybe your project isn't driven by cost. Maybe it's not driven by schedule. Maybe you want or need access to smart people all over the world.

In that case, look for smart teams, not individuals.

12.5 Hire Smart Teams, Not Solo People

The VP of Engineering who wanted to hire smart people all over the world had a good point. He should be able to hire those people and create better projects.

Instead of thinking about smart *people*, consider smart *teams*. Once you clarify the organization's and team's purpose, and you explain the outcomes that you want the team to consider, you might not have to do much more than let them loose on the problems you want them to solve. (See Consider These Innovation Leadership Principles on page 1.)

When you create feature teams that can finish their work as a team, you reduce the cycle time for that team. If that team is part of a program, and they can carve out relatively independent work, your program might cost less, too. (For more on program management, see *Agile and Lean Program Management: Scaling Collaboration Across the Organization* [ROT16A].)

Before you commit to people far away, consider creating a value stream map, as in the previous figure, and see how long the best-case cycle time might be. What if you hired a team of people? What if you decided to work north-south instead of east-west? What if you hired people with greater overlap time instead of lower salaries?

You have options if you want to hire people or teams that do not live in your geographical area. Make sure you have enough hours of overlap so you don't unintentionally create higher costs and personal frustration within the teams.

12.6 Options to Lower Cycle Time and Project Costs

You *can* create independent cross-functional teams that work on different products and use people all over the world. Especially if you want to create teams near your various customers. You will need to outfit the teams with sufficient tooling so they can communicate as necessary.

Even if teams start off independent, they rarely stay independent. As the products grow, the teams tend to become more interdependent.

You can create teams where the overall cost is lower if you choose to pay a salary based on the local cost of living. For example, at the time of this writing, based on numbers from salary.com, the cost of living in San Francisco is 62.5% higher than the U.S. national average. In Detroit, Michigan, it is 2.1% lower. If you are based in the U.S. and you set expectations well, you might be able to pay people fairly but not equally and save money on wages.

What if you're based in Europe or Asia? You might not want to use US knowledge workers—even if they live in Detroit. US salary expectations might be too high for you. However, you have many options for north-south hiring in Europe and Africa, and east-west hiring in Asia and eastern Europe, just as a start.

If you also feel pressure to deliver faster and cheaper, focus on cycle time for the team. Consider these options:

1. Ask your managers about the pressure they feel to reduce cost or project timelines. See if they have these short-term problems:
   - The tyranny of quarterly reporting, forcing managers to focus on the short-term, not the long term.
   - The perception, especially in the stock market, that lower wages mean lower project cost.
   - The need to capitalize the product as quickly as possible. Many managers don't realize that cycle time often has more influence on project cost—and the ability to capitalize the work—than the salary of any one person or team.

2. Visualize the cycle time for your current or proposed teams. What organizational obstacles can you remove to reduce the delays in your current teams?

3. If you have not yet hired people in various locations, consider where you might want to hire people to take advantage of expertise at lower salaries.

4. Make sure the people you hire want the same purpose and outcomes you do. If you do choose to outsource, consider asking for a project team that stays together for a minimum of six months.

5. If you already have people across the globe, ask the teams to see if they can create more hours of overlap to make a collaborative team.

6. Where possible, create independent feature teams wherever you've already hired people.

If you need to reduce the cost of development, start by reducing the cycle time. I addressed specific ideas about how teams can work together in Book 2. In addition, the more technical excellence the team uses, the faster the team can go. (See *Create Your Successful Agile Project: Collaborate, Measure, Estimate, Deliver* [ROT17].

If your managers want to hire lower-cost people as part of short-term thinking, start using cycle time as a way to guide your decisions. Sometimes, when we're in challenging financial times, it's difficult to plan for the long-term. You can hire people in various locations, as long as you realize the cycle time tradeoffs you're making.

If you want to hire people in various locations as a strategy, read *From Chaos to Successful Distributed Agile Teams: Collaborate to Deliver* [ROK19], for many more ideas for your distributed teams.

CHAPTER 13

Who Has the Power to Decide?

How many policies, procedures, and standards does your company have? Think about all these examples of decisions codified as policies, procedures, and standards:

- Accounts Payable for travel expenses.
- Administration for allowable furniture in the office—including the number and size of monitors.
- HR for when and how you can promote or reward people.

I've seen more:

- When managers sign off on work they don't participate in. You might have seen a "Change Control Board" composed of managers, not the peers of the people who do the work.
- When managers decide on core hours—not the team or the workgroup.
- When managers impose an "estimate" on a team and expect the team to deliver to that date.
- When managers decide on any process they don't use themselves. For example, when managers decide which approach or framework a team will use.

When I ask people if there's a name for these policies, procedures, and standards, they almost always say, "Bureaucracy!"

Many of these policies arose because we want to prevent Something Bad from happening. Or, someone did Something Bad long ago. That person might have paid for the infraction. The policies, procedures, and standards still punish the people in the organization.

These policies, procedures, and standards reinforce the status quo and can make innovation quite difficult. In addition, the policies, procedures, and standards reinforce hierarchical and centralized decision-making.

And, while managers can try to enforce a hierarchical and centralized approach to decisions, people talk to each other. Any given team or workgroup understands how they work and how they finish work.

And, if the people work on an overarching goal? They talk to each other as in Figure 1.4: Small-World Network on page 15.

Why do managers make decisions for other people? Often out of fear, such as the risk that someone will make a mistake and that mistake will have significant consequences.

The people with the organizational power make those decisions. And, too often in my experience, the people who decide do not have to live with their decisions. Here are some examples:

- An international company had policies that anyone VP level or above could fly business class for international flights over five hours. The technical staff had to fly coach and did not have an opportunity to arrive a day early to catch up on sleep. At least 80% of the time, the technical staff had to discuss and decide on the product issues—not the managers.
- A company that wanted to manage their real estate footprint decided only managers would have offices—even though the managers rarely used their offices because they traveled so much.
- A company often advanced loans and other low-cost money perks to their managers. The technical staff waited weeks for travel reimbursement.

The result? The managers had plenty of autonomy. The technical staff had very little autonomy.

When managers make decisions like these, managers reinforce their power. Power is not good or bad—it is a fact. The question is, who uses which power?

I see many problems with policies, procedures, and standards:

- The more policies and procedures your organization has, the less experimentation and change you can encourage. The fewer experiments you can tolerate.
- The policy is often outdated and does not achieve its desired result.
- We rarely examine and remove outdated policies.
- Too often, the people who make the decisions do not have to live with the result of those decisions.

The policies, procedures, and standards reinforce management power. When managers don't relinquish power, people have to ask the manager for permission. That increases cycle time and too often creates underprivileged people and teams.

Management power tends to increase management control.

With decision power, managers tend to create a culture that stifles innovation, autonomy, and mastery. We don't optimize for the organization's purpose, the overarching goal. Instead, we reinforce resource efficiency, not flow efficiency.

Standardization—via policies and procedures—can strike anywhere in the organization. And, in my experience, the more policies and procedures you have, the more policies and procedures you create.

Back when I was a programmer, I had a boss who wanted to create coding standards. He'd heard all of us developers whining and complaining we couldn't read the code. He got tired of listening to the whining. He wanted us to be able to read each other's code. He created coding standards—by himself—so he wouldn't have to hear us complain anymore.

One Monday morning, he handed each of us a three-ring binder with at least 50 pages of coding standards. He'd tried to address all the particulars for this programming language—tabs vs spaces, how to name variables, and how long certain methods could be. We were supposed to follow these standards to the letter.

I was appalled. I looked around the office. Everyone else had the same look on their faces.

We all agreed something would have to be done. I was part of the six-person group who made an appointment with him. We walked in.

He smiled. "Is this a mutiny?"

In my ever career-limiting fashion, I said, "It might be."

Everyone laughed. Including our boss.

We explained that since he wasn't going to write code, he wasn't the right person to set the standards. He could tell us the results he wanted. We would deliver those results.

My boss was happy we decided to stop whining and act. We created four pages of guidelines that would make one person's code easier for others to read. While we didn't all like everything, we used limited consensus to make sure we could live with everything. We all adhered to the guidelines. And yes, the code became much easier to read.

Coding standards are just one form of policy that assumes there is a single standard way to work. Coding *guidelines* allowed us to make it easy for other people to read the code.

Guidelines and constraints often produce better results than standardization.

13.1 Myth: I Can Standardize How Other People Work

Joseph, the CIO, smiled. "Okay, I'm really glad we can start this management meeting now. It's time to talk about standardization. I want to create standards for our projects. I want to standardize on a single agile approach for all of our projects. I think you'll all be pleased. Teams won't be going off in every direction. We can standardize once and for all."

Cathy, the QA director, wrinkled her forehead. "Uh, Joseph, are you telling us you want us to go 'all in' on that one agile approach right now?" she asked.

"Sure. Why not?"

"Well, we haven't finished our pilot project, for one thing, and we don't have enough money budgeted for training," Dave, the Development Director, said. "And while I think an agile approach is a great way to go for many projects, our business counterparts have to think so, too. We need to bring them with us. Right now, they're still thinking in six-month or year-long chunks. You can't standardize on any agile approach without changing how they think."

Joseph raised an eyebrow.

"Why do you care how we deliver, anyway, as long as we deliver effectively?" Cathy asked. "Our job is to solve problems. Your job is to make sure we are solving the right problems. If you decide which problems we solve by managing the project portfolio, we can decide how to solve the problems."

Dave continued. "What if we decide that we need to prototype some architecture for a while to reduce technical risk? Are you going to have my head?"

Joseph looked at Dave for a minute, then said, "No, I'm not. But I thought you liked that agile approach."

"I do," Dave said. "But the developers and I don't quite understand refactoring to patterns at the architecture scale that we have. We're working at it."

Cathy nodded. "That's the same way my team doesn't always understand how to create tests and refactor to test automation all in one iteration."

"Transitioning to any agile approach—or any other approach— isn't a slam dunk just because you declare it," Dave continued. "It's a change."

"And why should we use just one approach?" Cathy asked. "Why shouldn't we iterate on architectures or designs for a while if we want to? What's wrong with that? And what about trying flow and WIP limits instead of formal iterations? Why can't we do that? Why do we have to standardize on anything? Why can't we experiment and see the results of our experiments? We need to learn from our pilot and experiments."

Dave said, "I feel as if we are finally getting out of the yoke of waterfall. I don't want to be back in the yoke of something I don't understand. You hired me because I can think. I hired people because they can think. So did everyone else in this room. It's time we let them think about *how* they do their work, not just *what* they do."

"Forget the idea of standardization," Cathy added. "Our projects are different from each other. Why should we use the same approach on each project?"

Joseph took a breath and looked as if he was about to say something.

Cathy held up her hand. "Let's tell people the results we want and use a weekly or biweekly cadence to make sure we get the results in a reasonable amount of time. Why do we have to do more than that?"

Joseph leaned back in his chair. "Okay, as long as you reflect on your experiments and fix them when they go wrong, you have a deal."

13.2 Standards Create a False Sense of Security

A "standard" approach to anything offers people—especially managers who don't do that work—a false sense of security. They assume that a standard will force the work to proceed smoothly. How often does that happen? Not often enough!

You can standardize work on an assembly line and make the work safer and more efficient. But knowledge work? When you standardize knowledge work, you run the risk of making the work less innovative, less efficient, and not oriented to the real goal of your project.

Standardization for knowledge work might *look* efficient. However, standardization is often not effective. That's because knowledge work has many unknowns and we can't fully plan for those unknowns.

Since we can't fully plan, we need to adapt our plans as we proceed based on more information. The best way to adapt the plans is to work with others in flow efficiency and create short feedback cycles to see our new reality. And, if teams have all the information they need, they can solve problems as a team.

As Don Reinertsen said in *The Principles of Product Development Flow: Second Generation Lean Product Development* [REI09]:

"Decentralizing control requires decentralizing both the authority to make decisions and the information required to make these decisions correctly."

If managers have all the authority and information, the teams can't make good decisions.

We have many principles for finishing work. When each team decides together, they can use the best of all the options. The team does need to know its overarching goal and all the necessary information to do great work.

When the team knows what they need to accomplish and they have control over their work, they have enough autonomy to improve their work.

13.3 Imposing a Standard Removes Autonomy

Except for safety or regulatory requirements, I have yet to see a reason to impose a standard on someone else's work—especially if a manager does so. Even then, the people doing the work might see ways to be safe and live inside the regulations.

When managers impose standards, they implicitly say, "I don't trust you to do your jobs. Here. I will tell you how to work in detail." Do you want to do your job that way? I don't.

I actually like *my* constraints on my work. I like deadlines, as long as I can decide on the scope. For example, I often live with dates and word count when I write articles for other people. Not only can I live with constraints as constraints, I often find it a fun challenge to see what I can do inside those constraints.

There's a difference between telling someone how to do a job and providing constraints around the outcome.

When you tell people how to work, you might get malicious obedience. (Once, when I had to fill out a timesheet and limit the time to 40 hours, I stopped working overtime. My boss wasn't happy, although I became much healthier because I paid attention to everything I had to do outside of work.)

When you explain the constraints, people can choose how to do the job.

But when managers told me how to do my job, I didn't live with that very well. I always thought of ways I could do it better. Always.

I often tried the work their way. Too often, it took me too long, or I couldn't get the outcomes we wanted. I finally got permission to do the work my way. I asked for guidelines and the necessary constraints. I got them.

Some of my managers were surprised by how well my approaches worked. That's because I was in the code or the tests or the project. I had the context. I knew the people. The managers were too far removed to be able to offer specific advice.

The people you lead and serve also know their work better than you do. That's their job.

I like to think about the work—the approach and the work itself. I bet the people you lead and serve do, also.

13.4 Policies and Procedures Prevent People from Thinking

Managers create policies and standards to cover a multitude of past sins. Too often, when managers see "bad" or challenging behavior, they want a policy to prevent recurrence of that behavior. Instead, they could offer feedback about why that behavior doesn't work for the organization.

Worse, many standards try to cover all of the potential problems in a process. The standard wants to prevent people from thinking. That's how we got to big, honking binders of process.

The people who write the process binders read them. Other people rarely do. And, that's when we don't update the processes. We create brittle working systems.

13.5 Standards Create Brittle Systems

How much adaptability and resilience do you need in your organization? Adaptability is the ability to recognize a change and create alternatives to the current way we work. Resilience is the ability to capitalize on any of those alternatives.

Too often, standards create systems that discourage adaptability. The less often we practice adaptability, the less likely we are to be adaptable. And, the less often we try to change anything, the less resilience we have because we haven't practiced.

The more we try to mandate how people work, the fewer options people have to make choices. Fewer options means people experiment less often. Without learning from mistakes as well as successes, we can't build resilience in organizations.

Why do we hire people? To think and solve problems. Do we ever *not* want people to think? No. We want people to think. We want people to think hard. We want people to solve problems, whether it is with the process or the product.

We hired these people because we thought they were smart. They are. Let them show us how they apply their problem-solving skills to the project itself, not just the problem domain.

Sometimes, the people doing the work don't know how to solve the problem. That's when managers can go "meta" and address the environment that prevents people from solving the problem.

13.6 Power Derives from Decisions (and Hierarchy)

The people in power make the decisions. The more managers decide for other people, the more the managers reinforce their power. And, the less trust they create with the people the managers lead and serve. With less trust comes less autonomy. After a while, people behave according to the environment. (See Environment Shapes Everyone's Behavior on page 10.)

Why would managers make decisions for people?

Every single time a higher-level manager says to someone down the hierarchy, "You're responsible for this deliverable," that higher-level manager reinforces a culture of hierarchical power dynamics.

I often see this kind of decision-making when, instead of starting with a large corporate objective as in Verify the Team's Objectives on page 61, the manager has a personal objective for some sort of delivery. Even though managers don't deliver—the people doing the work deliver.

Managers do have a superpower here—they can create an environment where people can safely be transparent about their work, their concerns, and the policies themselves.

Managers can create guidelines and constraints.

13.7 Guidelines and Constraints Build Adaptability and Resilience

No one can foresee all the possible problems and plan for them. I have seen many organizations where, with the use of guidelines and constraints, people solved problems the standards did not anticipate.

Have you ever tried to change a standard? Every time, I see a ton of cost in time and meetings.

Standards reinforce the status quo. If you want more innovation, see how you can move from standards to guidelines and constraints.

Back in Book 1, I said the cost of changing a management decision reflected the adaptability and resilience of your management system. How adaptable and resilient do you want your organization to be?

Guidelines and constraints help people solve problems themselves. If they can't solve the problem, they'll come to you for help in some way. I said this in Book 2:

Managers lead when they create a team that can solve problems where those problems exist.

When you extend power to the people doing the work, you can create a more innovative and resilient organization.

Consider these guidelines or constraints inside an organization:

- People can spend money up to a certain amount per quarter or per year. They can spend that money on a new computer, training, a conference, whatever. They have the autonomy to spend that money and receive reimbursement.
- Teams can organize around the work the way they choose to, as long as they deliver something everyone can see at least once a week (or so), or as long as they are available to the customers when the company needs them available.
- Teams decide when they take vacation time. No one needs to ask a manager. (If everyone wants to take the same week off, what can you, as a manager, ask the team to do to manage those risks? That's where working in flow efficiency helps teams and managers.)
- Teams can create projects to address the unfinished work they incurred from the way they worked before. (Managers can then look at the cycle time savings in doing this work.)
- Teams can decide who gets promoted—and who doesn't. (See Must We Manage Performance? on page 39.)

I bet at least one of these might scare you. Especially the last one about teams deciding on promotions. That might be the first step to open-book management. And, you, and all of your management peers, would then also need to be transparent about your salaries.

Guidelines build the culture of "the way we do things here." Once those ways become part of the culture, you don't need standards. People see useful ideas and extend those as long as they have safety and transparency.

13.8 **Create a Safe and Transparent Environment**

When I think about moving from standards and policies to guidelines and constraints, I ask these questions:

- How little can the manager decide *for* the team?
- What results, framed in guidelines and constraints, might you request?
- If some manager says they need to decide for a team, ask: What three alternatives have you considered so you don't have to take the team's power away?

Make it possible for people to think and deliver, rather than working by rote.

When I worked with Joseph, the CIO in the story at the beginning of this chapter, I asked him what he wanted from his agile transformation.

He said, "I don't actually care how the teams work. I want to release something that works every single week and doesn't break anything. That will give us time to finish enough projects and get everyone off my back. I can't support all the products. I can't hire more people. I want to finish enough so I can manage my demand management."

Demand management is another way to describe the project portfolio.

He defined the guideline and constraint: Release something every week. Make sure that thing works and doesn't break anything else.

I suggested he tell his directors and the entire organization that goal. He could then specify the guideline: release something every week, and the constraints: don't break anything else. Once he did, some teams used the agile approach he'd wanted to standardize on. More teams used a combination of recognizable agile approaches. And, several teams created their own approach, based more on technical practices than project practices.

It took several months, but the teams finally started delivering finished features. Joseph did find some relief from the constant demands. He was able to instill more adaptability in the IT department, and with his colleagues across the organization.

You might need different guidelines—all based on the problems you want to solve. For example, if you say:

- "Manage cash outlay for travel expenses." Remote teams might decide to move their quarterly meeting to a different location. They might choose to move the dates of their meetings. They might ask customers to consider a different time or date.
- "Help us manage our real estate footprint." Some teams might choose to work primarily remotely. Others might choose to work mostly in a team room. Others might suggest a different metropolitan area that has lower real estate costs.
- "Help us see when teams might complete a project so we can tell the customers." Teams can measure their cycle time. They might show you how interruptions change their ability to forecast. They might have suggestions for tooling and automation that would help them deliver something small next week.

When you ask people to decide based on *outcomes*, they will create possibilities you didn't know existed. All because you created safety so they could be transparent.

Managers need to decide how much transparency they can tolerate. In my experience, the more policies, procedures, and standards you have, the less transparency you have.

13.9 Options to Address Decision Power

The more policies you have, the more fragile and brittle the system of work becomes. (See *Antifragile: Things That Gain from Disorder* [TAL12] for more details.) The more decisions you make, the less able other people are to make decisions.

Think about your current business. Ask yourself these questions:

1. How complex is your environment? Do you have more ambiguity than you prefer? Do you have many interdependent variables, all creating more unknowns than you like?
2. How much change do you want to accommodate in the business, to change who you want as customers or which products you offer?
3. Do you have products where you need to use lean startup experiments?

If you said, "Yes" to any of these questions, you have a less predictable business environment. The less predictable your business environment, the more you can use guidelines and constraints to help people make better decisions faster.

Do consider sharing decision-making power. Every time I started sharing more decision-making power, I felt as if I was working without a safety net. I asked people to help me:

1. How can we make it possible to learn early without crashing our business?
2. What other information do you need so you can make good decisions?
3. Do you see alternatives I don't see?

The more I discussed these questions, the more I realized I could trust the people to do the work. They knew more than I did about their context.

If you do need to make decisions for others, ask yourself these questions:

1. How many of your current policies, procedures, and standards can you throw away? I often discover that organizations add to their policies and never remove them. Can you select three policies, procedures, or standards to remove?

2. If you need policies, can you give the people who need to live with these policies a say in creating them?
3. When can you offer people guidelines and constraints within which to do their work, as opposed to a policy, procedure, or standard?
4. Can you explain your thinking to help people see what to do and what not to do?

CHAPTER 14

Isn't the Organization a Well-Oiled Machine?

Years ago, I worked for a company planning a move to a new building several miles away. The current building had small areas of cubicles, separated by walls. Functional teams sat together in these areas. Each functional team had several whiteboards in their area. We used those whiteboards to model, design, and discuss. We often had the benefit of people not on our project overhearing the discussion and adding to our knowledge. Sometimes, a couple of developers visited the test area—and vice versa. We all learned from those conversations.

The new building had an open floor plan. Instead of large whiteboards on the walls in the various areas, the building architect and senior management decided the teams could meet in conference rooms, which would have whiteboards on each wall. In addition, the hallways would have whiteboards.

We would have plenty of whiteboard space to use in our discussions—but not where people had their computers and other work artifacts.

Why all the changes? We needed more space, which is why we planned to move. The new building didn't have smaller areas—all the space was open. And, the building architect and senior management didn't want the entire organization to hear the discussions in Engineering.

In the old building, you could walk by the various functional teams. Each team had its own personality, and we could hear that personality. Sometimes, the team was relatively quiet—and relative was the operative word. The whiteboard discussions occurred at varying decibels—which was fine with the engineering staff.

And, because teams gathered around those whiteboards to discuss options, and we were noisy, the building architect and the management decided the whiteboards had to go.

I started to plan the Engineering group's move—about 80 people and associated lab space. I was worried about several things: no refrigerator for lunches in the new kitchen area and no whiteboards in offices.

I approached the senior manager in charge of the move. I explained my concerns.

He said, "People don't need whiteboards in their offices. Besides, they work in cubes. We need to keep the noise down."

"They already work in cubes, just in smaller areas," I said. "Only the managers have offices. If it's noisy now, it will be noisier later with more people in smaller cubes. But, we can make that noise work for us, if we allow whiteboards so people can discuss design decisions in public."

"You don't understand," he told me. "Look, here's the noise level data in the Engineering areas now." He showed me his spreadsheet of decibel levels. "And, here's the data that says how many decibels of quiet people need to work." He showed me another spreadsheet.

I nodded. "I don't understand how no whiteboards will change things," I said.

"When people have to go to a conference room for discussions, they'll get the people they need and go. They won't disturb other people. The organization will be a quiet, well-oiled machine."

"That's not how engineers work," I said. "The more discussion we have—especially in public—the better the design is. Or the solution. Or the tests. People need to discuss in larger groups than one-on-one." I told him about how one team discussed their work with another team in the kitchen and solved both team's problems. "I hope that the open area will work like that."

He looked at me and sneered. "No. I've made a final decision. No white boards in offices. No cold drinks in the coffee room. We want people at their desks, working. I'm planning to measure how much time people spend at their desks."

Okay. My experiential data was not going to win against his spreadsheet.

When managers make decisions that affect how well people can do their jobs without any data from the people, they make less-than-useful decisions. I left that organization before the move.

While I like data to guide my management decisions, you can't put *everything* into a spreadsheet. That's a mechanistic approach to management.

And, if you do try to measure *everything*, you will get what you measure. (See Manage for Effectiveness on page 7 for the story about developers and testers gaming the measurement system for their own rewards.)

Mechanistic management doesn't work for any innovative organization.

Too often, managers who think the organization is a well-oiled machine think people are the problem.

No, people are the *solution*. People innovate. People imagine multiple possibilities. People are resourceful and brilliant problem solvers. People create the products and services we use and need.

Management is all about people. It's time to embrace the "messiness" that people bring.

Some of us aren't easy to get along with. Some of us are at places in our lives where we need a little help from the organization or our teams so we can support our parents, children, or the dog. Some of us want to advance as far as we can in our careers and some want to do a good job and call it a day.

That's why management is all about people.

It's true, I'm an optimist. In my experience, people want to do a great job. They want to learn, to master new skills. When I treat people with respect, when I maintain my integrity and the integrity of the organization, people show me what they can do. I'm always amazed by what people, with a common goal and respect for each other, can do.

14.1 Myth: I Can Manage by Spreadsheet

Susan, an Engineering Director, was ready for her one-on-one with her new VP, Dan. Dan had started just three weeks ago. The senior managers had hired Dan and none of the Directors had interviewed him. Three weeks and this was her first one-on-one.

Susan was a little worried about how Dan managed and what Dan was doing. She never saw him talk to people—people doing the work or his managers. She'd peeked into his calendar—no one-on-ones.

Well, she'd see what he had to say.

She knocked at his door and he motioned her to come on in. She sat at his visitor's table. He stayed at his computer.

He glanced at her. "You're sitting all the way over there?" he asked.

"Where else would I sit?"

"Across from me, so I can easily share this data with you," he said.

Shrugging, Susan walked over to one of the two chairs in front of his desk. She put her paper and pen in front of her, and put her glass of water to the side.

"Careful of the water," he said. "My machine is here."

"Yup, I can tell," she said.

"Like sarcasm?" he asked.

"I do!" Susan said and grinned.

He turned back to his spreadsheet and made a mark in it. "Okay. Ready. What do you want to talk about?"

Susan didn't think this was an auspicious beginning, but she was ready. "I want to know where we are with the plans for the new building. I want to make sure we have plenty of team rooms, or at least, rooms where people can collaborate."

"Here's what I was thinking," Dan said. "The teams who have the highest productivity get the biggest team rooms. And, the people with the highest productivity get private offices." He smiled.

Susan sat there, stunned. "What do you mean 'highest?' and what do you mean 'biggest?' I don't understand your thinking. You can't talk about personal productivity in an agile environment. You can't even talk about it in waterfall. We need an entire team to deliver the product. What do you want to know?"

Dan sighed. "I went back through the electronic boards and collected all this data. That's what I spent the last three weeks doing."

"Did you notice that all the data there is several months old?" Susan asked.

"Yes, I meant to ask you about that. Why aren't people updating the tools?"

"Because most of the teams work together," she said. "They started to pair, swarm, and mob as a regular thing because they get so much more done. They either use paper boards or a list on the wall. They don't track individual work because they don't work as individuals." She paused. "Even if they do work solo, it still doesn't make any sense to look at one person's work."

Dan looked at his spreadsheet and frowned. "That's okay, I'll get the new data."

"Look, do you think you can even assess us, your managers, as individuals?"

Dan nodded. "Sure, I can."

"No, you can't," Susan said. "I collaborate with my peers. We manage the project portfolio when we need to, to keep the projects on track and accommodate the various emergencies because the Operations committee never acknowledges those emergencies. We keep the teams going. We, as a management team."

Dan looked at her and leaned back. "Well, maybe you want to see my spreadsheet for product performance."

"Sure," she said. "What do you mean by performance?"

"How well the product made money for us over the past month."

"Month?" Susan asked. "That's not enough time for some of our products to find their footing. And, why are you doing that? Why not ask the Marketing or Sales VPs for their assessments?"

"Because they'll just focus on what they think, not what the data says."

Susan took a deep breath. "You're not giving those guys enough credit. Why do you think you have better data? I agree, all you VPs need to agree on the company direction, what the customers have paid for, and where you want the company to go. But, you don't need to generate your own data. If you can't trust your peers, who can you trust?"

Dan stroked his chin. "Good point."

"And, you need to trust us, your managers," Susan said. "We have data and you can see the data that people have in their retrospectives or in their improvement boards. You don't need to reward people based on what you think their productivity is. You need to smooth the way for them."

Dan sat back and crossed his arms. "I don't understand."

"We don't give people numeric goals," Susan said. "We use OKRs, remember?"

He nodded.

"Some of our objectives seem impossible," Susan said. "That's okay. We know that we can pick away at the goal until we either see how to do it, or realize we've met the laws of physics. But, we don't put numbers on people or teams. We haven't found that effective."

Dan said, "No? How do you calculate ROI?"

"We don't," Susan said. "We tend to use lean metrics for managing the day-to-day work. We have to report cost accounting measures, but we don't *manage* with cost accounting." Susan paused. "Why did you take this job?" she asked.

"Because I believe in this suite of products," he said. "I want to help the organization work to serve our current customers. I think that with a little more work, we can become a powerhouse in the industry."

"Good," Susan said. "I want that, too. I have ideas. All of the directors have ideas about how to accomplish that. I bet some of the team members have ideas, too. Why not start the discussions and create OKRs for how to get there?"

"Because I can trust my spreadsheets. Numbers don't lie."

Susan laughed. "Sure they do! They lie all the time. If we don't think about cost of delay and only look at estimates, we don't choose the right work to do. Cycle time and lead time don't lie, and a bunch of defect measurements don't lie, but cost to fix a defect lies. That's because we try to reduce the risks with the way we work. If a defect gets past us, it costs more to fix. Numbers lie all the time. The key is the context."

Dan leaned forward. "Take a look at these attendance figures for your teams." He pointed to the screen. "What's going on with Jane? We're paying her full time but she hasn't been working full time."

"I have an agreement with HR for this month," Susan said. "While she's getting her parents resettled in their new home, she has flexible hours. You're only counting the number of hours she's in the office. You don't see when she's working from home. Actually, she's gotten a ton done from home, even with flexible hours. I want more people to be able to work from home."

"How can I see the effect of her working from home?" Dan asked.

"Cycle time," Susan said. "Let me show you what her team finished just this past week." Susan took the keyboard and showed Dan the project wiki where the team discussed their previous completions and what they still had to do.

"But, all of this is qualitative data," Dan said.

"So? What's the problem with that?"

"I can't fit it into my spreadsheet."

Susan closed her eyes and took a deep breath. What were the senior managers thinking when they hired this guy? "Okay, here's the deal. We're going to talk about trusting people and teams, what OKRs are, and how our agile approach actually works and where it doesn't. We need to bring you up to speed. When do you want to talk with all the directors, or do you want more one-on-ones first?"

"You really think I'm wrong in my approach?" Dan asked.

"Dead wrong," Susan said. "Not wrong for wanting a dashboard. Not even wrong for wanting quantitative numbers. But wrong for not trusting us, your managers. Wrong for not trusting your peers. Wrong for not listening and investigating before you make decisions. And, wrong for not at least looking at the culture." She paused. "Yeah, wrong."

"Well, good that you told me how you really feel," he said and smiled. "I want to see your data, but don't expect me to change my mind. Let's go get me some information."

14.2 Embrace Management "Messiness"

We are humans, not automatons. People have good days and bad days. Some people succeed on one team and "fail" on another. That's because each team has its own environment. (See Environment Shapes Everyone's Behavior on page 10.)

However, no organization can create their products and services without people.

That means that while spreadsheets and other data are useful, they can't be the only way managers make decisions or manage.

Managers need to *see* how people work, not just *measure* how they work or their output. The organization needs achievements, outcomes, and results, not just effort. Too many spreadsheets manage effort.

14.3 Data Helps Management Decisions

Managers need data to make good decisions. And, our assumptions color the data we gather.

One manager, Stan, dutifully gathered story point data for his agile teams. He hoped when teams committed to more points, they would finish more work.

The teams did commit to more points. And, they finished less and less work.

I suggested he measure cycle time. When he did, he realized the teams did estimate their work pretty well. However, they had no idea that they had significant wait states and bottlenecks inside each team and between teams.

Stan's assumption was that story points were a reasonable gauge of what a team could do. He didn't realize cycle time was a much better indicator.

Managers need quantitative data to see the system: where are the bottlenecks? Where are the delays? Who inflicts most of the delays? Often, managers inflict delays when they don't make decisions early enough or fast enough.

Managers also need qualitative data. How satisfied are people with their jobs? How many and what kind of impediments do people and teams have? Are people generating new ideas for the products and services that get ignored?

I've seen this pattern in management many times: it appears that the senior managers work in a different context than everyone else in the hierarchy. The senior managers make decisions that make little or no sense.

You may have heard of the "WTF[1] quotient" as an organizational measurement. That's the number of decisions managers at any level make that confuse or abuse the people who do the work.

Managers might not always make good decisions or explain those decisions all the time, but the closer the WTF quotient is to zero, the better.

---

[1] WTF stands for Whiskey Tango Foxtrot as a polite way of saying "What The F***?"

14.4 **Consider Measures that Enhance Innovation**

Can you measure innovation? Maybe. You might find these measures helpful to create an environment that manages *for* change and refines the organization's "why."

Consider these possible measures:

- If you want an environment of collaboration, measure product lead time: how long does it take your organization to release an entire product? The lower the overall time, the better.
- If you want an innovative environment, measure the number of experiments you tried and what people learned. I'm not talking about supposedly *successful* experiments where you got the outcome you wanted. Instead, how fast can you learn? The learning is the value. So, the sheer number of team-led experiments might be an indication of the innovations of the organization.
- If you want to see how well managers enable the teams, consider measuring the wait time for management decisions. I regularly see managers take months or even years to decide to fund a project. Then, they ask the team(s) to finish the work fast. The teams start off "late" through no fault of their own.
- If you want an environment where people feel as if they can take responsibility, measure the number of times managers have to get involved with decisions.

This last measure is neither good nor bad. Sometimes, when managers impose decisions on other people, the managers remove autonomy. (See Imposing a Standard Removes Autonomy on page 143.) And, when managers don't set guidelines and constraints—when the managers are too laissez faire—the people often can't deliver the outcomes anyone needs. There is some middle ground. (Kurt Lewin called this "democratic" management.)

In my experience, if you want to encourage innovation, ensure the people doing the work have the ability to decide about the work.

The more management makes decisions *for* other people, the less innovative the people can be.

You might not like any of these measures. You'll notice that only one measure, the lead time, looks as if it might lead to revenue. All of these measures look at the flow of work through the organization—and the impediments to that work.

That's because an innovative organization experiences obliquity—not a direct path to a specific outcome, but achieving those necessary outcomes via oblique work. See *Obliquity: Why Our Goals Are Best Achieved Indirectly* [KAY10] for more information.

As product outcomes, you might measure:

- How many customers did we acquire, lose, or retain with the most recent release? (If we're not acquiring and retaining customers, our business will die.)
- Which products and services bring in what percentage of revenue? (Is that where we want our organization to go?)
- What profit did we gain on our revenue? (We need to make enough money on our investment in the work.)
- What's our cash flow (income and expenses), in the last month and last quarter? (If we don't manage our cash flow, it will manage us and restrict our options.)

These measures might be wrong for you. What else can you measure that would make a difference for your innovation?

Spreadsheets can help managers see the data. And, management is all about people.

14.5 Management is All About People

At dinner one night, after working at one of my high-school jobs, I proudly announced to my parents, "I know what's wrong with work."

My father asked, "Oh? What?"

I said, "People."

I didn't get to say the rest of what I wanted to say because the two of them laughed so hard they almost fell off their chairs. Neither of them could speak for what seemed like hours. I'm sure it was at least several minutes.

My mother continued to laugh. My father managed to ask, "Is that all? Why?"

I was a little puzzled. Yes, I was a little geeky back then. "Because people aren't deterministic. We can't ever have a well-oiled machine as an organization."

At that point, my mother said, "I don't know about this deterministic business, but no, organizations are not well-oiled machines."

I'm pretty sure they continued to laugh about what I said until they went to bed that night.

For years, many people thought that if we incentivized, motivated, or somehow carrot-and-sticked people, they would behave in deterministic ways. We could create an organization that looked like a well-oiled machine.

Let's forget about this well-oiled machine idea. Let's embrace the "messiness" of dealing with people and creating a great environment for them so they can work as well as they can.

With great management, you can accomplish great things.

14.6 **Options to Create an Opportunistic Culture**

When managers use spreadsheets, they often want to capitalize on opportunities. Here are some ways we can create a high-integrity opportunistic culture:

1. Clarify the overarching goal, the Outcome if you use OKRs.
2. Encourage collaboration at all levels to finish work.
3. Release that work to gain feedback as soon as you can.

When you let people know what outcomes you want, you create an environment where they can collaborate and they release their work. Then you can see and create opportunities. You might use spreadsheets, but you won't have to manage by spreadsheet. And, while your organization might look chaotic, it will actually be closer to that "well-oiled machine" you might want.

For knowledge workers, a well-oiled machine is about a cadence of useful delivery, not adherence to specific interim metrics.

I recommend you also review the principles in Consider These Innovation Leadership Principles on page 1.

CHAPTER 15

Where's the Quick Fix or Silver Bullet?

If you're like most of the managers I know, you feel tremendous pressure to deliver. Or, to increase sales. Or, to decrease support costs. The operative word is pressure.

Some of my clients have said:

1. If I just use a specific tool or change to another tool, I'll know where the project is.
2. If I just find a quick fix, we can paper over the problems. I won't have to take time to fix the issues.
3. If I just move to a specific agile framework, we'll get all the projects done faster.

Each of these sentences requires a culture change. The first sentence refers to project transparency. The second sentence refers to valuing proactive work. The third sentence infers the organization will change the entire culture to one of collaboration to deliver something small to learn and encourage change.

And, there's something similar in each sentence. Notice the "just" in each sentence. The word "just" diminishes the entire idea of cultural change.

Cultural change might require different tools. You might think you need a quick fix—or several—to make the changes stick.

We change the culture by changing our behaviors. What keeps the culture in place now? How can we address how we treat each other, what we can discuss, and what we reward if we want change?

I have yet to see a tool, a fix, or a framework change an organization's culture. We change our culture by changing our behaviors, and we change our behaviors by changing our habits.

Quick fixes and silver bullets don't change habits.

15.1 Myth: We Need a Quick Fix or a Silver Bullet

Dave, the VP, gathered his directors. "We need to go agile. Our profits are down. We can't release anything fast enough. Our customers are angry. We need to make money. We need to go agile."

Sherry, the Development Director, looked around. She said, "We need to be able to release more often. That's true. An agile approach might give us that. But I suspect you've got 'silver bullet' thinking. Agile approaches require cultural change. Are you willing to change our culture?"

"Absolutely!" Dave responded.

"So, you'll rank our projects and manage our project portfolio for at least a month at a time," Sherry said. "You'll stop moving people around teams. We'll pay off some of our technical debt to make our quality what it needs to be. You'll stop hiring onesies and twosies of people worldwide and hire feature teams if you really need to hire people off-campus. All of us have change lists a mile long that we want to address."

Everyone nodded. Terry, the QA Director, said, "My list might be two miles long." Some people laughed at that.

Sherry continued, "I'm all for transforming to an agile culture. But an agile culture is a long-term commitment to change. Are you sure you want that? It's not a short-term fix. What business results do you really want?" Sherry looked at Dave.

Dave looked at his directors. They looked back. No smiles.

"I want some predictability in my projects," he said. "I want to be able to release. I want to know that when I say to my peers that the software is ready to ship, it is ready to ship. I'm tired of not knowing anything."

"We can help you do that," Sherry said. "We can do all of that. We can do it with agility. We can do it with waterfall, but it would be more difficult. We can do it any way you want it. But you need to do your part."

Dave cocked his head to the left. "What's my part?"

"We didn't get this way in a month or three months," Sherry said. "We have 'emergencies' up the wazoo. You hire people all over the world, which could be a good thing, but the way you do it makes no sense for the teams we have. Right now, the way you hire people makes everything take longer."

"But I'm saving money on salaries," Dave said.

"No, you're not," Sherry said. "You only tell us once you've hired these people, and we have to integrate these people into our work. We're the ones who have to get up at four A.M. or stay late until seven or eight P.M. to make the time zone differences work. You tell us there's no money for travel to bring these people up to speed, but you don't hire people with the skills we need. It's nuts. Our cycle time gets longer and longer."

Dave's shoulders slumped. "I thought I was helping. You need more people to do the work."

"Look," Sherry said, "if we were involved in the hiring decisions, we might be able to make it work. But that's not even the worst part. You, the management team, and the PMO can't decide from week to week what the top-priority project is, and yet you want us to budget yearly. We have to multitask to get anything done. What we do makes no sense at all."

Dave cocked his head to the right. He looked as if he was listening intently.

Sherry took a deep breath. "We have really talented people working here. We have systemic problems that arise from years of ignoring those problems."

Dave sighed.

Sherry continued. "We have tons of technical debt—we're running fast just to stay in place on that. I don't know what to tell you. We can do anything you want, but we aren't going to turn this organization around in a month or two just because you want us to. 'Agile' is not a quick fix. It's not a silver bullet. We don't have anything resembling an agile culture. Have you tried to get a purchase order for something we need? It takes months, and there's no transparency."

Dave started to speak.

Sherry held up her hand. "I'm not trying to complain. I'm not. I'm explaining where we are. What project do you want to release first? Maybe that's the best place to start. If we release that, maybe we can get some breathing room."

15.2 Know Your Business Reason for Any Change

I see too many managers want to use agile approaches because "agile has crossed the chasm" or because "it's the right thing to do" or because "everyone else is." Many people use the agile words. Too few organizations live the agile values.

That means few organizations that attempt an agile transformation truly change their culture. Culture change takes time, and it changes almost every aspect of the organization.

Most of these organizations bounced back to something else. That something else didn't look anything like an agile approach.

Quick fixes and silver bullets don't create lasting changes in behaviors. What happens when the manager who championed the change leaves?

- People stop using the tools.
- People revert to the old behaviors.
- Worse, the rewards never changed, so even if people see the value in new behaviors, they have no reason to change.

In all cases, the people revert to how they worked before. In the case of an agile transformation, the organization can't sustain the necessary culture changes.

As with every potential change, you need to know why you want to change. Do the business reasons support the changes you want to make? Is the organization ready to support the change? If not, what does the organization have to do to prepare for that change?

15.3 There is No Quick Fix or Silver Bullet for Culture

Remember the conversation at the start of this chapter about an agile approach not being a quick fix? Some people, especially senior managers, think that a specific approach or framework or tool will cure all the ills of your organization.

The problem is that a new project approach or a new tool is neither a quick fix nor a silver bullet. People need time to learn about the new approach or the new tool.

Organizations have culture problems because the people—often with best intentions—created the culture. You can't fix culture problems fast.

That's because Environment Shapes Everyone's Behavior on page 10. Your environment—the system of work—creates and can fix these problems.

Are tools or approaches useless? No! The problem is that a new approach or a new tool isn't enough. That's because Dr. Paul Batalden[1] was correct when he said:

"*Every system is perfectly designed to get the results it gets.*"

Along with a new approach or a new tool, you need support and management change. You need to change the environment that caused the problems in the first place.

15.4 Beware of Management Fads

I have enough tenure in this field to have been subjected to many management fads, all of which would supposedly "fix" our problems.

---

[1] https://www.psqh.com/julaug08/editor.html

Back when I was a programmer, I learned about structured design and was supposed to use it. Structured design was supposed to make our projects deliver on time.

When our project schedules were such a disaster, we were supposed to use Gantt charts to monitor the schedule. The one thing a Gantt chart tells you is the very first day you *can't* prove the project won't be done.

I went to Total Quality Management school, courtesy of one of my employers. Some of the principles were useful—especially the reasoning about waste. However, my employer chose to make us play baseball backward to show people how useful TQM was. (True story.)

Too many people in the software industry now use agile approaches as a management fad. They say, "This framework says to do this! If we do this every day, we'll be agile."

Agile approaches require cultural change. If you're willing to change your culture, they will help you see where you might make other choices. Agile approaches are a subset of lean thinking. I've suggested much lean thinking in this book.

When people think you're out for a quick fix, they know you're pitching a management fad. You don't need to follow the fads. Instead, offer meaning to people via the organization's purpose. And then, experiment.

15.5 Reframe Change as Experiments

Managers create and refine the culture as they create the environment in the organization.

If you want a quick fix or a silver bullet, consider these questions:

- How safe is it for you or anyone else to propose a change?
- How much does your organization reward learning, as opposed to a success?
- Does your organization reward change or even reward discussing change?

- If a change you propose "fails," what are the consequences?

Too many of my clients fear proposing changes. If they do propose a change, they often select something they think will be a safe change: a known tool, a specific framework, or something that fixes a customer problem but doesn't prevent the problem.

That's because too many of my clients work in places where the culture says, "We can't afford to fail." If you can't afford to fail, you can't afford to change.

And, if you do "fail," your career is never the same.

Reframe "Fail Fast" to Learn Early

When I think about failing, I think of an event with no way to recover. I hate that kind of failure. Too often, when other people hear "Fail Fast" they hear, "No way to recover from something bad."

Instead, reframe the idea of failing fast as a way to "Learn Early." I've started to ask the question, "How early can we learn and at how low a cost?"

When we reframe the fail-fast idea to learn early inexpensively, we can create small experiments we can learn from. We create experiments that align with the organization's purpose.

Some people say we should celebrate failure. I don't buy that. I will celebrate learning, especially if I can learn something fast.

Instead of failure, can you discuss experiments and learning?

How long has it been since you tried to change anything in your organization? If your organization isn't accustomed to changing often, any significant change will take longer than you might imagine.

If you want organizational change, try changing something *you* do first, rather than asking someone else to change first. You'll lead the change and see how difficult it is to change something.

Avoid naming the change something such as "Agile transformation." I recommend you not name a change at all. If you do need a name, consider "experiment" or "bet." When you experiment, you can create hypotheses, take measurements, and use the experimental loop for change. Bets might prompt you to create inexpensive experiments.

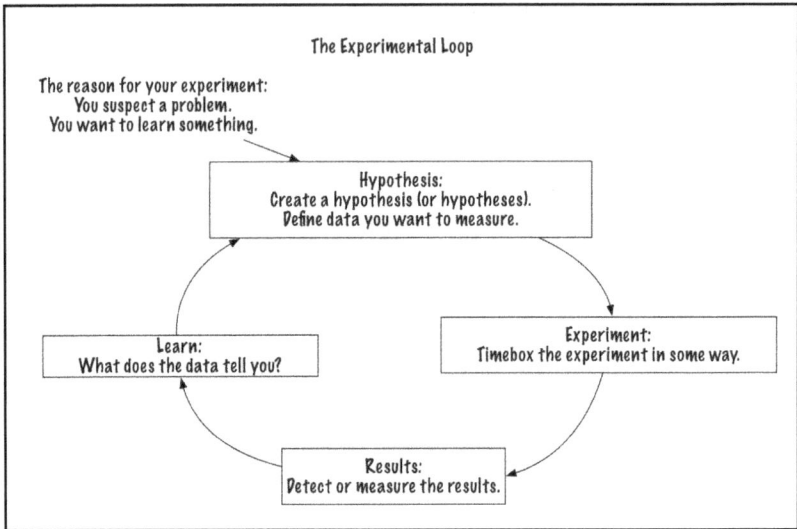

Figure 15.1: Experimental Loop

This is an experiment:

1. Write down your hypothesis.
2. Write down the data that will help you discover if the hypothesis is correct.
3. Create a system to measure that data.
4. Decide on how long the experiment should run (timebox).
5. Measure the results.
6. After you gather the results, determine what the data tells you.
7. Decide: Continue? Change? Stop the experiment?

Here's an example experiment one of my clients ran. The senior managers thought they should use a specific agile approach. The managers were concerned that the specific approach would actually take longer than what they were currently doing.

The hypothesis was that teams would be able to release features faster. The measurement was cycle time for each team.

The teams created two-week experiments and measured their cycle time. At first, the teams were slower. Each team had to manage the shortcut decisions they'd made earlier to release incomplete code and tests.

After the second two-week experiment, some of the teams picked up speed. Other teams realized they needed to change their agile approach.

As the teams experimented, they realized that releasing was easier because they practiced releasing more often. And, they automated much of the releasing work.

Some teams discovered that their features took much longer because they didn't have sufficient access to a product person. And, some of those teams didn't have sufficient test automation to support their work.

The culture slowly changed. Before these changes, the organization released too early and let the customers discover the problems. Then, the organization responded to emergencies.

As the teams changed how they worked, they had to respond to emergencies *and* change the way they worked. After about six months, they finally were able to show that this new way of working was faster and better for the customers.

The technical teams still required more change. And, the managers had to change their way of managing.

The managers made "failure" safe for the teams and the people. The managers started assuming the teams wouldn't succeed the first, second, or even the third time. The managers realized that the culture hadn't gotten this way overnight. That meant none of the changes would be fast. However, the changes would be worth it.

Changing a single habit or an entire culture takes time and effort.

15.6 **Options for Change**

Any significant change takes time. Sometimes, small changes take time, too.

I recommend you first read Esther Derby's *7 Rules for Positive, Productive Change: Micro Shifts, Macro Results* [DER19]. Any change is personal for you, every single person you serve, and every person you influence. Derby's seven rules may offer you opportunities for conversation. That conversation will provide you with much more value than a quick fix or a silver bullet.

1. Make sure you Encourage Flow Efficiency on page 12 at all levels—especially with the management teams—before anything else.
2. Limit the Work in Progress (WIP) for the entire organization. (See *Manage Your Project Portfolio: Increase Your Capacity and Finish More Projects* [ROT16].) That will help you reduce the organizational pressure for more work.
3. Review your rewards system and make it easy for people to experiment and learn from their work.
4. Encourage retrospectives and reflections at all levels all the time. If everyone works to improve the same small thing each week, you'll improve as an organization.

Keep assessing the entire system. As problems continue to arise—and they will—you will discover new behaviors or habits you need to change. Experiment to fix those. That's how you can eventually change the entire culture of the organization.

CHAPTER 16

Where Will You Start Leading an Innovative Organization?

I hope you decided to read this book to create a culture that invites change—not for change's sake, but to create a culture of innovation.

And, you might wonder if your organization requires innovation.

16.1 Does Your Organization Require Innovation?

Think about how work has changed in just the past 20 years. Back in the late 1990s, we still had secretaries who supported departments. And, some managers still had secretaries print out email so the manager could scribble something on paper for the secretary to mail back.

Twenty years ago, most of us had land lines or "dumb" cell phones. Now, "everyone" uses a smartphone.

Today's smartphones have *significantly* more computing power, memory, and storage than almost any computer back in the early 2000s.

There have been many more technology changes you might find even more important. We changed the products and some of our technical capabilities. And, our management practices have not kept pace with how we *can* work now.

In *The Mortality of Companies* [DAE15], researchers reported that a publicly traded company can expect to survive about a decade. That's because other companies acquire a company. Or, the company splits or merges with a different company. Or, the company dies because the organization couldn't innovate or change—either in its products or its processes.

I can't guarantee *when* your company will need to innovate. I do know you will need to innovate at some point.

And, as I said, I'm writing this book in the spring of 2020, when COVID-19 has created the need for each of us to reassess everything about our companies and our management.

The more you consider the ideas in this book, the more you create an environment in which people can collaborate, and the more you will be able to innovate.

If you've read this far, you realize that leading an innovative organization requires collaboration at all levels. Where will you start your journey?

As with all management efforts, start with yourself, with your level of influence.

How can you create your part of the organization to optimize for innovation? How can you use the innovation principles to create a culture where people contribute to the whole?

16.2 Reinforce a Culture of Innovation

Cultures that foster innovation apply the innovation principles in these ways:

1. The people at all levels understand why they work on this project, this product, this service. They are proud of how they contribute to the greater whole.
2. The managers limit the organizational WIP by deciding on the project portfolio. The managers consciously decide what to do first, second, third, and never.
3. The managers seek outcomes. Some of those outcomes are "failed" experiments—because we couldn't deliver the work, but we learned from our efforts. And, the managers don't

criminalize failure, because they see the value in the learning everyone experiences.

4. The managers believe in flow efficiency for teams, and especially for managers. When managers have a common goal, they reduce decision time, and the managers encourage teams to work together.

5. The managers encourage relationships among people across the organization. The managers realize the technical people have eureka moments when they talk with each other rather than compete with each other.

6. The managers limit the number of policies, procedures, and standards. The managers use principles, guidelines, and constraints to encourage the behavior they want to see, not criminalize behaviors the managers don't want to see.

7. The managers encourage change and experimentation in everything—the process, the products and services, even the business model.

8. The organization creates transparency around goals, deliverables, and how the business works.

What would you have to do for your team, your group, your department, your company to live the innovation principles? What actions do you need to reinforce, remove, or change?

When I consciously wanted to become more innovative, I learned to collaborate with my colleagues, so we could Encourage Management Flow Efficiency on page 12. We learned to make decisions faster, decisions that elevated the "Why," as in Start With Why on page 4.

We looked for outcomes at all times, and visual progress. We found that when we encouraged people across the organization to interact and to challenge each other, the culture became even more innovative.

In a real sense, we moved to egoless management. (I first learned about egoless programming from *The Psychology of Computer Programming, Silver Anniversary ed* [WEI15].)

I wasn't perfect and neither were my colleagues. However, we practiced managing *for* innovation.

I reconsidered my management practices. I hope you do, too.

16.3 Assess Your Current Actions

Consider your current behaviors and see if you want to experiment with them:

- In what ways do you clarify the organization's purpose? Or, this product's purpose?
- In what ways do you manage for effectiveness, not efficiency?
- How do you encourage outcomes, not outputs?
- How do you encourage people to learn about other people and what those other people do across the organization?
- In what ways do you reinforce organizational integrity with the least number of guidelines and constraints for the people?
- In what ways do you experiment, yourself?
- How do you make your decisions transparent?

These behaviors are about how you live the innovation principles.

I'm not perfect. You don't have to be either. And, when you start with yourself first, you're more likely to achieve what you want.

16.4 Change Your Behaviors First

Choose something as your experiment. I chose the project portfolio when I was a manager. I wanted to manage it for effectiveness and outcomes. I was tired of multitasking and I was tired of asking people to multitask. I knew I was asking them to do less than their best work.

I've had to fight to do the right thing. As you can tell from my stories in these books, I don't have problems challenging others to do what creates integrity. I'm not you. You will need to choose your own actions.

You might choose another of the innovation principles. You might start with experiments. Or, maybe you'll start by making your decisions more transparent.

Wherever you start with your behaviors, find allies. The more allies you enlist, the more you'll work in management flow efficiency, and the more likely you are to succeed.

16.5 You Don't Have to be Perfect

Remember the goal of managing for innovation—to create an environment where people can experiment and learn. Where people expect change, not dread it.

You might not be able to say, "We're going to be innovative now and change everything." Even I might look askance at that statement.

Consider how you can start to create a culture of innovation now:

- How do you collaborate with your peers so you can work in flow efficiency?
- How can you define meaningful outcomes?
- How can you create an environment where everyone can contribute, where people welcome innovation and change?

You might not see change quickly. In fact, if your organization hates the idea of change, you might not see any change at all for a while. You can continue to practice in your part of the organization.

When you focus on the long term and work on your integrity and congruence, you are more likely to gain the effects you want.

We cannot be perfect, especially when we want to create an environment that supports innovation. We depend on too many other people and we make mistakes. That's why revisiting the ideas in Book 1 and Book 2 help so much when we want to lead an innovative organization.

I periodically examine my beliefs and actions to see if what I do helps or hurts my innovation.

I recommend you do the same.

16.6 Is an Innovation Culture For You?

After all this, you might wonder if it's worth your aggravation to create a culture of innovation. I like to think about the problems managers solve.

Great managers solve culture problems. And, culture problems are big, messy, systemic problems. You'll address something over here and something over there will break. You'll never run out of problems to solve.

Maintaining a culture of integrity might be the most challenging job a manager can do. Managers feel pressure, and the pressure is real. Your culture can aid your work.

The more you collaborate with others, the more options you can generate to solve these problems. Remember the Rule of Three back in Increase Management Capability on page 27? One solution is a trap, two solutions is a dilemma, and three possibilities breaks logjam thinking, helping people think of more possibilities. I use the Rule of Three to practice making my management better and better.

Work with your cohort—your peers at your level and your colleagues across, up, and down the organization—to create an innovative organization.

I hope you enjoy your management journey.

Annotated Bibliography

[BAT15] Bateson, Nora. *Symmathesy: A Word in Progress*. At https://norabateson.wordpress.com/2015/11/03/symmathesy-a-word-in-progress/. Provocative ways to think about how people work and learn together. Includes ways to think about why you might not attempt a divide-and-conquer strategy for the people and the work.

[HAM07] Hamel, Gary with Bill Breen. *The Future of Management*. Harvard Business School Press. 2007. If you haven't considered how to innovate in your practice of management, this is an excellent book to start thinking about how to do so.

[HOF03] Hope, Jeremy and Robin Fraser, *Beyond Budgeting: How Managers Can Break Free from the Annual Performance Trap* (Harvard Business Press, 2003). The classic text about how we can rethink salaries and budgeting.

[DAE15] Daepp, Madeleine I. G., Marcus J. Hamilton , Geoffrey B. West and Luís M. A. Bettencourt. *The mortality of companies*. Published in *Journal of the Royal Society Interface*. 2015. Find the source at https://doi.org/10.1098/rsif.2015.0120. A fascinating look at the typical half-life of a publicly traded company.

[DER19] Derby, Esther. *7 Rules for Positive, Productive Change: Micro Shifts, Macro Results*. Berrett-Koehler Publishers, Inc. Oakland, CA. 2019. There's a lot to like about this book. And, what I like best is this: the openings for the various conversations you need if you want to change something. When we think about ourselves, the other, and the context, we can create conversations that matter. Those conversations will allow you to create change that matters.

[DOE18] Doerr, John. *Measure What Matters: How Google, Bono, and the Gates Foundation Rock the World with OKRs.* Penguin. 2018. The original text on OKRs, Objectives and Key Results. OKRs are not MBOs, Management by Objectives. Instead, OKRs talk about the outcomes the organization wants to achieve.

[DRU01] Drucker, Peter. *The Essential Drucker.* Harper Collins, New York, 2001. If you haven't read all 30+ of Drucker's books, this book is a great distillation.

[DWE07] Dweck, Carol. *Mindset: The New Psychology of Success.* Ballantine Books, New York, 2007. This book discusses the fixed mindset and the growth mindset. If you have the fixed mindset, you believe you can only do what you were born with. If you have the growth mindset, you believe you can acquire new skills and learn. The growth mindset allows you to improve, a little at a time.

[EDM12] Edmondson, Amy C. *Teaming: How Organizations Learn, Innovate, and Compete in the Knowledge Economy.* Jossey-Bass, San Francisco, 2012. How self-organized teams really work, and what we need to make them work in different cultures.

[HEL19] Helfand, Heidi. *Dynamic Reteaming: The Art and Wisdom of Changing Teams.* 2019. A fascinating look at how teams can get stale, become rigid, and how you, as a leader, might nurture reteaming in your organization.

[HHM10] Hofstede, Geert, Gert Jan Hofstede and Michael Minkov. *Cultures and Organizations Software of the Mind: Intercultural Cooperation and Its Importance for Survival, 3rd ed.* McGraw Hill. New York. 2010. Hofstede proposes our cultures program our minds. A fascinating look at how organizations (and countries) create and reinforce their cultures.

[KAH11] Kahneman, Daniel. *Thinking Fast and Slow*. Farrar, Straus and Giroux. 2011. Many of us (including me) think we understand how we think. Not so fast. In this classic text, learn all the various thinking traps and fallacies.

[KAY10] Kay, John. *Obliquity: Why Our Goals Are Best Achieved Indirectly*. Penguin. 2011. We often fall into the trap of a direct approach to complex goals. This book explains why an indirect—an oblique—approach may be much better.

[LEN00] Lencioni Patrick. *The Four Obsessions of an Extraordinary Executive*. Jossey-Bass. San Franciso. 2000. Effective executive teams learn and act together. So do all other management teams.

[MAM15] Mamoli, Sandy and David Mole. *Creating Great Teams: How Self-Selection Lets People Excel*. The Pragmatic Bookshelf, Raleigh, NC. 2015. Yes, you can facilitate people choosing their own teams and it works.

[MOA13] Modig, Niklas and Pär Åhlström. *This is Lean: Resolving the Efficiency Paradox*. Rheologica Publishing, 2013. Possibly the best book about how managers should consider agile and lean. A wonderful discussion of resource efficiency vs. flow efficiency.

[PIN11] Pink, Dan. *Drive: The Surprising Truth About What Motivates Us*. Riverhead Books. 2011. All motivation is intrinsic: autonomy, mastery, and purpose. Once people believe they are paid fairly, it's all about autonomy, mastery, and purpose.

[PFS06] Pfeffer, Jeffrey and Robert I. Sutton, *Hard Facts, Dangerous Half-Truths And Total Nonsense: Profiting From Evidence-based Management* (Boston: Harvard Business School Press, 2006). If you don't believe me, read this book. Two Stanford professors who can actually write. What a treat.

[REI09] Reinertsen, Donald G. *The Principles of Product Development Flow: Second Generation Lean Product Development*. Celeritas

Publishing, Redondo Beach, CA, 2009. A classic for understanding lean principles applied to product development.

[BCD05] Rothman, Johanna and Esther Derby. *Behind Closed Doors: Secrets of Great Management.* Pragmatic Bookshelf, Dallas, TX and Raleigh, NC, 2005. We describe the Rule of Three and many other management approaches and techniques in here.

[ROT07] Rothman, Johanna. *Manage It! Your Guide to Modern, Pragmatic Project Management.* Pragmatic Bookshelf, Dallas, TX and Raleigh, NC, 2007. If you want to know more about how to estimate task size, establish a project rhythm, or see a project dashboard, this is the book for you. I have references about why multitasking is crazy in here.

[ROT12] Rothman, Johanna. *Hiring Geeks That Fit.* Practical Ink, 2012. Learn to hire people, from writing a job description to a great first day. All the templates are available for free on Johanna's website. The book explains how to use them.

[ROT16] Rothman, Johanna. *Manage Your Project Portfolio: Increase Your Capacity and Finish More Projects, 2nd ed.* Pragmatic Bookshelf, Dallas, TX and Raleigh, NC, 2016. Sometimes, program managers encounter project portfolio decisions with the feature set, or the request for people to multitask. This book helps you manage all the work in your project portfolio. I also have more references about why multitasking is crazy in here.

[ROT17] Rothman, Johanna. *Create Your Successful Agile Project: Collaborate, Measure, Estimate, Deliver.* You don't need to adopt a specific framework for any given agile project. Instead, use the agile and lean principles to adjust for your project's context.

[ROT16A] Rothman, Johanna. *Agile and Lean Program Management: Scaling Collaboration Across the Organization.* Practical Ink, 2016. A program is a collection of projects with one business objective, often requiring several feature teams. Learn how to scale the collaboration, not the process.

[ROT15] Rothman, Johanna. *Predicting the Unpredictable: Pragmatic Approaches to Estimating Project Schedule or Cost.* Practical Ink, 2015. What you need to know about estimation and what to do when your estimate is wrong.

[ROK19] Rothman, Johanna and Mark Kilby. *From Chaos to Successful Distributed Agile Teams: Collaborate to Deliver.* Practical Ink. 2019. Learn the principles so you can make your distributed agile team successful.

[SAN13] Sandberg, Sheryl. *Lean In: Women, Work, and the Will to Lead.* Alfred Knopf. 2013. If you haven't read this book, do consider it. I especially liked the jungle gym metaphor for careers.

[SHI08] Shirky, Clay. *Here Comes Everybody: The Power of Organizing with Organizations.* Penguin Books, New York, 2008. Why collaboration works, even when people don't know each other. It's fascinating. Where I first learned the term "small-world networks."

[SIN09] Sinek, Simon. *Start With Why: How Great Leaders Inspire Everyone to Take Action.* Penguin. 2009. Stories and the reasons about why purpose matters more than anything else.

[TAL12] Taleb, Nassim Nicholas. *Antifragile: Things That Gain from Disorder.* Random House Publishing Group. 2012. The core idea is the more resilient we can make our organizations (and ourselves), the less fragile we are. It's not an easy book to read. However, the larger our span of influence, the more we need antifragility.

[VAC18] Vacanti, Daniel S. *When Will It Be Done?.* ActionableAgile Press. 2018. Instead of estimates, consider forecasts. Not only will people start to appreciate the unknowns, you will discover you can create better small-item estimates and longer forecasts. He discusses the Aging chart, which is a way to calculate cycle time and lead time.

[WEI15] Weinberg, Gerald M. *The Psychology of Computer Programming, Silver Anniversary ed.* 2015. If you have not read this book and you work in the software field, read it. I first learned about egoless programming from this book. That learning has informed my actions— even if I couldn't always live up to my goals for myself.

[WOD16] Wodtke, Christina. *Radical Focus: Achieving Your Most Important Goals with Objectives and Key Results.* 2016. A business fable that clearly explains OKRs.

More from Johanna

I consult, speak, and train about all aspects of managing product development. I provide frank advice for your tough problems—often with a little humor.

If you liked this book, you might also like the other books I've written: https://www.jrothman.com/books/:

Practical Ways to Manage Yourself: Modern Management Made Easy, Book 1

Practical Ways to Lead and Serve—Manage—Others: Modern Management Made Easy, Book 2

Practical Ways to Lead an Innovative Organization: Modern Management Made Easy, Book 3

Write a Conference Proposal the Conference Wants and Accepts

From Chaos to Successful Distributed Agile Teams: Collaborate to Deliver

Create Your Successful Agile Project: Collaborate, Measure, Estimate, Deliver

Manage Your Project Portfolio: Increase Your Capacity and Finish More Projects, 2nd ed

Agile and Lean Program Management: Scaling Collaboration Across the Organization

Diving for Hidden Treasures: Uncovering the Cost of Delay Your Project Portfolio

Predicting the Unpredictable: Pragmatic Approaches to Estimating Project Cost or Schedule

Project Portfolio Tips: Twelve Ideas for Focusing on the Work You Need to Start & Finish

Manage Your Job Search

Hiring Geeks That Fit

Manage It!: Your Guide to Modern, Pragmatic Project Management

Behind Closed Doors: Secrets of Great Management

In addition, I have essays in:

Readings for Problem-Solving Leadership

Center Enter Turn Sustain: Essays on Change Artistry

I'd like to stay in touch with you. If you don't already subscribe, please sign up for my email newsletter, the Pragmatic Manager, on my website https://www.jrothman.com. Please do invite me to connect with you on LinkedIn, or follow me on Twitter, @johannarothman.

I would love to know what you think of this book. If you write a review of it somewhere, please let me know. Thanks!

—Johanna

Index

What Readers Are Saying About
Modern Management Made Easy Books

"The lessons I learned reading *Modern Management Made Easy* books make me a better leader. Descriptive examples paint a clear picture of situations at work I often find myself in, and applying the practical advice helps me better serve myself, my team, and my organization. Johanna influenced me to think congruently, and provided the tools needed to excel in my role. I can't recommend these books highly enough."

— Carl Hume, VP Engineering at Homestars

"If you are starting a new management role, or simply want a reminder of what it is all about, then these books provide a body of practical wisdom in an easily digestible form. They place the role of the manager in a wider context rather that implying some context free set of qualities and manage to avoid the platitudes all too common in books of this kind."

—Dave Snowden, Chief Scientific Officer, Cognitive Edge

"Do you need real-world answers to real-world management problems, especially to address agility at all levels? As I read Johanna Rothman's *Modern Management Made Easy* books, I nodded along and said, "I've seen that!" Use these books with their suggestions for what you can do to solve your real-world management problems."

— Scott Seivwright, Agile Coach and Leadership Pirate

"This series of books is a rare mix of personal stories, practical examples, researched theory, and direct calls-to-action. Rarer still, Johanna's writing segues between them without losing the reader or breaking their immersion. Whether you are a manager, an aspiring manager, or a coach of managers, these books will give you the necessary tools to develop new skills and the language to develop new cultures."

— Evan Leybourn, Co-Founder, Business Agility Institute

"Think of these books like three friends who can offer you advice on your management journey. You'll return to them whenever you want advice, reassurance, challenge, or renewal. I added these books to my library, right next to the late Russell Ackoff's books on the F/laws of management. Use these books to create your modern management and an environment that brings out the best in the people you lead and serve."

—Claude Emond, Organizational Performance-Growth Expert

"This book series is the furthest thing from your run-of-the-mill boring management books. Johanna Rothman busts dozens of management myths in an easy to read set of essays that are useful in part or as a whole. The stories and anecdotes told are relatable, practical, and fit for today's modern workplace. Regardless of your management experience, there's valuable lessons to be found on every single page."

—Ryan Dorrell, Co-Founder, AgileThought

"These books provide a wealth of practical leadership and team-building information. Project managers and leaders of problem-solving teams are often taught logical but flawed guidance from the industrial era. Today's project teams require servant leadership, inspiration, and collaboration skills far more than centralized planning or progress tracking. Johanna's books identify and bring to life better alternatives for undertaking challenging projects. Laid out in a helpful sequence, they provide a wealth of practical tools for today's practitioner searching for better outcomes and more satisfied stakeholders."

—Mike Griffiths, CEO, Leading Answers Inc.

www.ingramcontent.com/pod-product-compliance
Lightning Source LLC
Chambersburg PA
CBHW062130020426
42335CB00013B/1160